SDA 2.95

GALÁPAGOS

A Creationist Visits Darwin's Islands

By Lester E. Harris, Jr.

Illustrated by Robert Nipp

Southern Publishing Association
Nashville, Tennessee

Library of
Congress
Catalog Card
No. 76-23727

SBN 8127-0125-9

This book was
Edited by
Gerald Wheeler
Designed by
Dean Tucker

Cover photo by
Ernest S. Booth

Type:
11/13 Palatino

Printed in
U.S.A.

CONTENTS

The Enchanted Islands

The Pacific Ocean stretches in all directions around us clear to the horizon. The only thing we can see other than water and sky is our second small fishing boat about half a mile away. Its mast tilts back and forth as the little ship plows steadily through the swells. We've been traveling along together toward Tower Island since two o'clock this morning. It's now four o'clock in the afternoon, and we should have seen the island several hours ago. Where is it? Did we miss it altogether? I hope not, because it's a long way to Panama straight ahead in the direction we're going. Our captain has no charts and only a small compass to guide us. He's perplexed—and we're scared. We don't have much water, only a little food left, and fuel enough for one more day's traveling. Now we understand the meaning of the Spanish seaman's name for the group of islands—"Las Islas Encantadas," the Enchanted Islands.

There, way off to our left, is a thin silver-gray strip right down on the horizon. I can't even see it, but others with younger, sharper eyes do. That's our island. We turn toward it. The rays of the hot equatorial sun and the mist that daily hovers around and through the islands had hidden it completely, and we passed it by. Even now it appears to dance closer, then farther away. It will take us two hours to get there. The sailors of the old Spanish galleons were superstitious about the islands and stayed away from them. Galápagos Islands is a better name. The Spanish gave it that name too. It means "tortoise." Because of the giant land tortoises and their unique location, the islands have long been famous. Their greatest claim to fame, though, results from Charles Darwin's visit here in the fall of 1835 on the H.M.S. *Beagle*.

The Incas probably discovered the Galápagos Islands in the late 1400's. The first real records date from 1535 when tricky ocean currents swept the bishop of Panama, Tomás de Berlanga, five hundred miles off his course as he traveled from Panama to Peru. He wrote to Carlos, the emperor of Spain, about his visit here. The large iguanas on the shoreside rocks living on seaweeds, the tameness of the many species of birds, the thousands of giant tortoises, particularly impressed the bishop. He told his emperor that so many volcanic stones lay everywhere throughout the islands that it seemed to him God must have showered them down.

In the 1600's British buccaneers preyed upon the Spanish treasure ships leaving the west coast of South America for Spain laden with Incan gold. The Galápagos Islands were a perfect place to sail off to with their booty. Here they could find water in two or three places, and wood and meat were abundant. They turned goats, cattle, pigs, cats, and dogs loose on the islands to recapture in time of need. The animals soon went wild so completely that they began to replace the rare animals and plants found only here. Thousands of the once-domestic animals overran the islands. They ate the giant tortoises' food and eggs.

The tortoises must have been a popular source of food and water, for in a few years their numbers dropped from hundreds of thousands to a few thousand located only on certain of the islands today. On board ship the tortoises needed little care beyond a daily wash-down with seawater. They'd stay alive a year or so lying on their backs. Captain Porter of the U.S. frigate *Essex* tells of loading on fourteen tons of tortoises in four days. When the wind did not blow, a sailing ship might have to wait several weeks before it could move on. In the meantime, its crew would run out of supplies of food and water. It was then that they made the most of the big tortoises. The bladders of the tortoises held a gallon, more or less, of drinkable water, and the meat provided food. During the last half of the 1800's, records report the capture of more than

100,000 tortoises. It's little wonder that they face extinction today.

Many interesting stories survive from the early days in the Galápagos Islands. Once a pirate ship captured a big Spanish ship loaded so heavy that it rode deep in the water, only to discover that it was full of jars of orange marmalade. They sailed the ship into a little cove on James Island, where they dumped all the marmalade overboard. The place bears the name Buccaneer Cove today, and you can still find pieces of those pottery marmalade jars. In 1709 a pirate ship, with Woodes Rogers as captain, rescued the real "Robinson Crusoe" (Alexander Selkirk) from Juan Fernández Island, went to Ecuador, sacked the city of Guayaquil, then fled to Galápagos to hide.

A map of the Galápagos Islands dated 1793 has on it the location of the world's strangest post office. It's a barrel on a post at a place now called Post Office Bay on Charles Island. The barrel has weathered and worn out several times since, but a replacement is still there. A beaten path goes back just a few feet from the beach to the barrel. They put a roof over the barrel and a small door in the side. Today, sailing yachts and sight-seeing ships stop there to let passengers drop letters in the barrel. Each ship picks up the letters for destinations in the direction it is going. Stuck all over the barrel are pieces of driftwood, each with the name of a ship on it. The name of Queen Elizabeth's *Britannia* is there, for Prince Philip is fond of the islands and has visited them a number of times to photograph their unique animals and plants. The name of

Commander Irving Johnson's clipper ship *Yankee* also appears on the barrel. Each year the commander used to sail around the world with groups of young people, always stopping here. One name is gone. Probably a souvenir seeker took it. It is that of Count von Luckner's famous ship *Sea Devil.* The count was a German submarine commander during World War I. He always took the crews off before sending the vessels to the bottom.

For all of their popularity, the Galápagos Islands are fearsome, rugged, rocky places that are really the tops of volcanic mountains rising 10,000 feet from the floor of the Pacific Ocean. Each big island has its crater in the center. Isabela Island has six huge ones. One, Volcano Wolf, rises 5,600 feet, over a mile high.

The islands have the mildest weather in the world. The cold Humboldt Current, or Peru Current, comes up the west coast of South America, swinging out to sea at Ecuador to the islands right on the equator. Penguins and fur seals can live here because of the cold water. The only rain comes when a warm current from Panama mixes with the cold water. Since it usually happens at Christmastime, people call it *El Niño,* or "the Holy Child." They consider the rains a special Christmas present from God. Sometimes it only rains once in four years or so. The island inhabitants collect the rainwater in tanks of every description, for it is almost the only fresh water available. The Galápagos Islands have no springs and no underground freshwater as we know it. The volcanic rock is too porous to hold water long. Usually the people drink a diluted seawater pumped from cracks deep in the earth.

The two most unique and different things about the Galápagos Islands are the unique types of plants and animals and the tameness of the animals. It's nice to swim as I did in the crystal clear salty sea with a wild sea lion accompanying you, begging to be scratched, playfully nuzzling and swimming circles around you. There's something heavenly about lying down to rest a few minutes as I did and having a couple of Darwin's finches walk around you on a closeup inspection tour, then pick at a mole on your side as though it were a seed. When a mockingbird suddenly swooshed in to land on my chest, he strutted up and down my length from chin to toe, examining every inch and cheeping little notes of excitement about the strange creature lying on the ground. Three Galápagos doves came scratching along down the trail and without a moment's hesitation walked up on my body. One pecked my shoelaces untied; another scratched at my belly button to see if he could uncover something good to eat; the third came right up onto my face and turned his head over sideways, staring down into my eye as if to say, "Hey, are you in there?" Such tameness has impressed everyone who has ever visited the islands, including the single person most responsible for their fame, Charles Darwin.

Darwin quickly noticed how the famous finches, since named after him, varied from island to island and yet differed only slightly from their nearest relatives on the mainland of South

America. He correctly reasoned that each species had developed right where we now find it. Using that bit of insight to the processes of natural variation and survival under rugged conditions, he went on to develop his ideas about nature into a theory which has totally altered man's thinking about himself and about all life.

I am in the Galápagos Islands to see the same things Darwin observed. To watch strange birds with stub wings. To sit beside the big albatross as it protects its single giant egg from the heat of the equatorial sun. To search out the different species of giant tortoises on the various islands. To watch marine iguanas carrying on their strange life on the edge of the sea. And I wonder. Didn't Darwin draw bigger conclusions from what he saw than he should have? Didn't he stick his neck out and guess that a lot more happened in nature than really took place? I think so. In the next chapters we'll look together at some of the strange and wonderful plants and animals in the Galápagos Islands to see what lessons God is trying to teach us by their ways of life.

Lizard of the Sea

Tuh! Tuh! Tuh! Tuh! The sound is all around me, even though the roar of the sea breaking on the jagged, pitted, lava boulders just below where I'm sitting almost drowns it out. Each noise comes from the nostrils of a black pug-nosed lizard. All together I guess five or six hundred lizards surround me on the flat, slanted rock. When I walked among them, they ran aside a few feet and paused to watch me. They don't seem really afraid, just cautious. I sat down among them to observe quietly for a while the only lizard in the world that lives in the tidal zone and grazes on algae at the bottom of the sea.

When I first approached the lizards, it startled

them so they snorted loudly, squirting directly at me a stream of salty water three or four feet from each nostril. Half-dollar-sized patches of wet appeared on my pants. I had read about their little trick and was prepared for it. Since the lizards spend a part of every day in the sea and drink seawater, which is full of salt, they must have some kind of special system to get rid of the salt. Most animals and man would quickly die if they drank seawater. Some birds and the marine iguanas, though, have special glands designed to remove the excess salt from their blood and dispose of it. One pair of the glands lies under the skin behind the eyes. Another pair is in the nostrils on each side of the head. They open into the nostrils where they continuously drip water about twice as salty as the sea. When alarmed, the lizard blasts the liquid out in two parallel squirts by forcefully blowing air through its nose. Most of the time the liquid simply drips out the nostril openings and evaporates, leaving behind a crust of sea salt. Sometimes little cones of salt jut out of each of the iguana's nostrils.

I settle down as comfortably as I can on the bare rock and watch the lizards. They average between two and three feet in length—large for lizards—and they're fat. (I never saw a skinny marine iguana anywhere in the islands.) Most of them weigh between four and ten pounds. Glancing around on neighboring flat rocks I can see maybe three thousand of the reptiles. Punta Espinosa on Fernandina Island has the largest single group of the creatures that Darwin called "imps of darkness." They congregate along the coast where lava reefs covered with algae lie just offshore. Conditions are ideal if low tide bares the reefs, but most often the really rich algal reefs occur about a hundred yards offshore at depths up to thirty-five feet. The iguanas also require a sandy- or loose-soil area where females can dig burrows in which to lay their eggs.

As the iguanas around me settle back down, several casually walk right up to me and plop down on their bellies on the hot rock. The heat radiating back off the rock makes the sweat pour down my face. Yet here is a cold-blooded reptile whose temperature is supposed to be the same as its immediate surroundings. Scientists have measured the temperature of the rocks up to 122 degrees Fahrenheit. If that of the lizard's rose that high it would probably die. How does it keep its temperature down? As I watch, I see the secret of its temperature control. It is now three o'clock in the afternoon, and the lizards have their bodies all pointed in the same direction—almost facing the sun. While it is hot, they orient their bodies in such a way that they expose only a minimum of their body surface to the sun and a maximum faces the onshore sea breezes that keep the air temperature at about 86 degrees. A high body temperature while they rest helps to digest the algae they eat.

The marine iguana has the greatest ability of any lizard to control its rate of temperature change both in the air and in the water. At night the iguana may choose to sleep right out on the exposed rocks, stretch out on a low limb of a dead mangrove tree, or crawl under a rock ledge or down into a crevice.

A black animal on black rock in the black of night is pretty safe anywhere.

In fact, the marine iguana has few enemies on land. But in the water it must watch out for the shark. Consequently it ventures out from shore only at feeding time. If you throw one into the sea, it will immediately make a dash for shore. On land, birds, crabs, sea lions, and even the Galápagos snake mingle with the iguanas. Young iguanas, however, have a number of enemies. The Galápagos hawk, Galápagos snake, lava and swallow-tailed gulls, yellow-crowned and black-crowned night herons, and lava herons will all feed on the small, fat-bodied, defenseless creatures.

Eating for a marine iguana is a highly specialized process for which their bodies are neatly adapted. For example, their toenails are long and curved and their legs are short and muscular, making it possible for the lizards to cling tightly to the rocks as they eat, despite giant waves washing over them. The tail, flattened sideways, the iguana uses as an oar to propel its body through the water. It never employs its legs in swimming but folds them close alongside the body. The lizard swims through the sea, head held high, at a good rate of speed.

Its teeth are uniquely different in their specialized design for grazing algae. Each tooth is flattened sideways and divided into three chisels—a long one in the middle and a shorter one on each side. Each row of teeth looks like a saw with its serrated edge. When the upper and lower jaws move opposite to each other, the teeth cut as effectively as the blade of a farmer's mowing machine. A short pug nose aids in getting large mouthfuls at a time, cutting short the actual time needed to graze and lessening the dangerous exposure to sharks.

One of the marine iguana's strangest characteristics is its ability to swim out to sea, dive down to the bottom in seventy-degree water, and feed. Such a temperature, twenty-five degrees lower than its land environment, would slow down any other reptile into total immobility. It is a real shock to a herpetologist (reptile scientist) to see a reptile sluggish at its highest environment temperature and most active at its lowest environment temperature. It simply does not happen for any other known reptile. The iguana grazes underwater for an hour or more, controlling its buoyancy in some unknown manner. A scuba diver must counterbalance his weight underwater with a belt to which he attaches five-pound lead weights. The marine iguana has been seen swallowing stones, which is perhaps how it manages to stay down so long. It can hover at any depth it chooses for any length of time it wants to. Studies by the famous marine zoologist Jacques Cousteau show that not only does the lizard not breathe while underwater, but its heart all but stops beating.

A few of the lizards may feed at any time during the day, but those I watched on Hood Island seemed to have built-in clocks which notified them exactly when it was time to go eat. It occurred precisely at the low tide nearest to noon. Day after day I watched the iguanas get up from their basking and begin to march down toward the sea from their high perches (some more than a hundred feet up in the seaside cliffs). They all moved at about the same instant. First one here and another there, then large numbers all together. Out to sea they went, leaving their basking rocks bare. It was uncanny to watch and wonder how a sluggish, sleeping animal could so accurately tell tide time.

In January the breeding season begins with male iguanas measuring out their home areas by butting and pushing each other around for four or five hours at a time. Cone-shaped scales cover the top of each head. When two lizards put their heads together, they sort of fit into each other in a nonslip fashion with the cones of one fitting into the low places in between on the other. Simultaneously each male will raise the spiny crest down the middle of his back and open his mouth wide to show its bright red inside. Finally one lizard wears the other one out. The loser simply lays down on his belly before the winner for a few minutes, then quietly slips away. The dominant male now guards his territory for about a week, not even bothering to eat during that time.

One male will court two or three females by rapidly bobbing his head up and down in front of each one. After mating, all go back to basking together on their favorite sunning rocks.

The females now start wandering off by twos and threes to the nesting ground. Each chooses a particular spot in the sand or dirt to dig her burrow. Any other female coming too close she vigorously butts away. The burrow is in the center of a circular territory about twenty feet across. She lays two big eggs, each tubular with rounded ends. Their shells are soft, leathery, white, and about two and a half inches long. After egg-laying, she seals the nest up. Reproduction ceases for the female until the next year. The eggs incubate two months and hatch. A horny knob—called the egg tooth—has developed on the end of the little lizard's nose. He slices the shell open by slashing from side to side against the inside. Crawling out and wriggling upward, the young reptile is soon free and on his own.

About the only parasites the iguana has are ticks. The lizard doesn't try to dislodge them. Nature, though, has provided another means of removing them. Two species of Darwin finch, the saucy Galápagos mockingbird, and even the Sally Lightfoot crabs pull the creatures off the basking iguanas.

The Mighty Sea Wanderer

The name *albatross* is magic to bird lovers and ancient seamen alike. An ornithologist (bird scientist) does not consider his life complete until he's had a chance to observe the albatross at home and in the air. Sailors, especially in the days of sailing ships, loved to have the superb birds wheel and circle around their vessels. It broke the monotony of long days at sea and also meant that good sailing was ahead, for the birds ventured out to sea only where the prevailing winds were best.

Once you see an albatross in the air, you will always recognize it again, for no other bird has such a great size combined with such long narrow wings. You can even see the big yellow hooked bill from some distance away. Everything about the albatross is impressive, but the effortless coasting through the air just above the water is like poetry in action. The albatross skims close to the waves, rising and dropping with them so easily that it's almost magic. The bird anticipates each action of the sea in advance. A fast-breaking whitecap never catches it off guard.

From a distance the big bird appears to almost lazily hang in the air. But as it comes closer to your boat, you suddenly realize that it's gliding by at an incredible speed for such a flimsy mass of flesh and feathers. William Beebe, a natural scientist who did much with his books to make the creatures of the Galápagos Islands popular, once stated, "The voice of a chanteuse [lady singer] and the flight of an albatross are among the more wonderful things in the world."

Some old-time sailors were superstitious about the albatross, thinking it bad luck to kill one because it possessed the spirit of some sailor washed overboard in a storm. On at least one occasion the bird brought good fortune though. A great albatross fell on the beach at Fremantle on the west coast of Australia. It had a tin tag around its neck with a message from the survivors of the French ship *Tamaris,* which had wrecked three weeks earlier. Thirteen of her crew had gotten to a remote Crozet island. A ship went there to rescue them. The big bird had flown over four thousand miles of open ocean with the tag around its neck, too terrified even to stop and eat.

Linnaeus, a great Swedish classifier of animals and plants, had so much respect for the albatross in flight that he labeled it *Diomedea exulans*. The name means the "God-counseled homeless one," as though the great bird needed special help in his long sojourns from solid land.

The Galápagos albatross will stay at sea for two years, rarely ever even landing on the water. Once touching down on the sea, though, it has a difficult time taking back off. The rougher the sea, the easier the albatross can become airborne by launching itself from the crest of a wave. For that reason the birds tend to stay more in the "Roaring Forties" latitudes below the equator where it is windy most of the time. A full-bellied bird may even have to regurgitate his food in order to lighten himself to regain the air.

Taking off from land is even more difficult than from the sea. And landing is a calamity. Gliding in over the nesting ground, the albatross must time its approach and regulate its speed exactly, in order to come anywhere near its nest. The long narrow wings have a high stalling speed, which means that as the bird slows down it simply ceases to fly while still in the air. It then plops in a head-over-heels crash. Big volcanic boulders all over the breeding-nesting ground add to the hazard. Majestically the big bird gets up, shakes its feathers smooth, and walks over to its nest with its head swaying from side to side. Beebe said an albatross walking looks like it has "flat feet, fallen arches, and crippled limbs." To take off on land, the bird needs a runway of at least a hundred feet of clear ground or a cliff from which it jumps in a falling arc to begin its incomparable soaring flight.

The male on a nest I have approached on Hood Island is becoming restless. I'm getting too close to him. He feels threatened. Gently I reach out toward his head. When he waggles that great hooked beak at me, I draw my hand back quickly. The large beak is one of the main characteristics of the Galápagos albatross. His body is a little smaller than the rest of the species, but even so he's as big as a large goose, though weighing only eight to ten pounds. His wings outstretched spread eight feet. Once again I try to stroke his smoky brown body. He lets me do it! It is a thrill to actually touch the rare wild bird in its native habitat.

Other men have not been so gentle. Lichen hunters have killed the birds with clubs and taken their eggs for food. I'm glad that Ecuador now protects the islands as a national park and that park officials carefully watch over this breeding area along with the one on the other side of the island, the only two places in the entire world where one can find the birds on land. Scientists estimate that only about 2,500 of the birds exist today.

The female standing nearby moves over to groom the male. She pays no attention to me as I settle back to watch. The male reaches over and touches her beak with his. The two then stand up and begin a remarkable display of motions and beak banging. It is most vigorous during the early part of the breeding season when the birds return to the nest site after their long sea sojourn. I feel fortunate to see even a little bit, for it is now late in the incubation season and the birds do not court frequently. The two albatrosses ignore me. They stand opposite each other and bob their heads from side to side in time with little sidestepping motions. Their beaks point downward as their heads turn back on their shoulders. Then they rub and click their bills together again. Suddenly they raise their beaks toward the sky and lower them quickly, clicking them fiercely against each other for thirty seconds or so. A deep, soft "go, go, go," uttered by both birds, follows the clicking. With slow bows they sit down facing each other. The female settles on the eggs, and the male begins grooming her. If only man were as tender and gentle to his fellows as the great birds are to each other.

The female albatross lays her half-pound, cinnamon-speckled eggs singly in early April. If the rainy season is early, mosquitoes may become so abundant and pestiferous in their attacks on the poor albatross that she will abandon her egg. The nest consists of nothing more than a bare place on the red earth in a clearing amid boulders and heavy brush about a hundred yards from the seaside cliff.

The newly hatched chick is a soft, puffy ball of brown down. The parents feed it two or three times a week. Leaving the chick, they sometimes go out to sea for several days to fill up on anchovies, squid, and herring. A special part of the albatross' stomach converts part of their food into an oily secretion which the parent pumps into the young bird on demand. The chick can hold as much as two quarts at once. Because of the weight of the food, he can't even stand up but wobbles on his knees.

By January the last of the young birds have matured enough to take off over the sea. They course up and down the great expanse of the Pacific Ocean from Panama to the south of Peru and stay out for three years while they grow up. They then return to the same breeding ground to raise their own family. Year after year a pair will keep returning to the same nest site. Their life-span covers about twenty years.

The sun sinks rapidly over the ocean. The big male of the nearby pair of albatrosses gets up. With neck leaning far to each side, he slowly walks toward the cliff. At the cliff his great wings extend. He looks almost afraid to jump. There's a little slope between two boulders. Running down between the rocks, he spreads his wings and is airborne without a single flap of his wings. Downhill he goes, building up speed. Around into the wind he circles to climb, then back with the wind in a long descent to the waves and food as the equatorial sun suddenly sinks below the sea. It is night. I return slowly along the cliff to my ship, marveling at what God has wrought in the magnificent Galápagos albatross.

Black Spooks of the Sea

It is almost dark. We have at last arrived at Tower Island. Our little fishing boat has churned steadily along since we left Santa Cruz Island at three o'clock in the morning. Once out of sight of Santa Cruz we continually scanned the horizon for sight of Tower. According to calculations we should have arrived here about two in the afternoon. It is now six. Our captain had gotten off course, and we had sailed right on past the eastern side of the island and toward Panama when one of our group spotted a narrow blue-gray line way off on the horizon to the left. After making a ninety-degree turn, in two hours we arrived at our destination. Ahead of us is an opening into the center of the island. The captain guides our ship into it. Inside, we see a cliff rising eighty to a hundred feet almost all of the way around us. We are in the middle of a mile-wide extinct volcano. Over our heads circle and swoop in intricate patterns of glide and dive at least four hundred "spooks of the sea." Frigate birds, or man-o'-wars, are one of the most unique kinds in all the world.

The water is choppy inside the volcano because the opening from the ocean is on the windward side. Our captain anchors both ends of the boat to keep it from drifting into the tumbled mass of boulders at the bottom of the cliff. Jagged rocks jut up from the water all around us. We're glad our captain knows his business, even if he did get off a little on his navigation. After all, he did it all by dead reckoning—a tiny compass and no charts. Going ashore in the dinghy, we climb out on a tiny beach of sand formed from the shells of crumbled mollusks and weathered volcanic rock. The black spooks swish down close to our heads to land on the surrounding shrubs. Eerie cries and calls echo off the cliff over to the right. Man-o'-war birds are everywhere. They hover a few feet over our heads, curiously watching us as we dare to invade the privacy of their roosting and nesting grounds. It's too dark to see much detail. The birds are so black that they hang overhead like pieces of a giant mobile, their strings stretching to the clouds, fluffy and rosy from the last rays of the setting sun.

Two things about them impress us: their large wingspan and their marvelous ability to do anything in the air they want to with hardly a single noticeable movement of their wings. The wings stretch out eight feet, yet the entire bird weighs only two or three pounds. The man-o'-war has the greatest ratio of wingspan to weight of any bird. They hold their narrow wings in a slightly pulled-in position while flying. Seeing one of the birds head on reminds you of an almost flattened-out W. As a flying machine, it is absolutely unparalleled in nature.

One morning at sea I awoke from sleeping on the deck to see a man-o'-war bird hovering just above the mast top directly over my head. There did not seem to be even the slightest breeze, yet the bird stayed in position without appearing to move a muscle as the boat traveled along. After about ten minutes he veered off with great speed to the sea's surface. Up and down he went, inches from the water, his dips perfectly synchronized with the rhythm of the waves.

Half the bird's weight consists of the wing feathers and flight muscles. Once it has landed, though, it has a terrible time trying to get back into the air. Consequently I have never seen one on the ground except along the top edge of a cliff where it can jump off to get airborne. At sea, the bird rarely ever lights on the water. One good reason is that it can't waterproof its feathers with oil like most other birds. As a result it would get so watersoaked that it would never be able to fly and would actually drown. Its legs and feet are used only for perching. They are too small and weak for walking or swimming. In a bushtop, the bird bounces a little to let the springiness of the shrub give it a boost when launching itself into the air. Once in the air, the man-o'-war can withstand strong winds. The "spook" can fly in hurricanes that will beat the pelican into the sea.

Though we class the man-o'-war as a seabird, it really is a better thief than fisherman. Occasionally it will snatch a flying fish out of the air or eat a young seabird or the eggs of another species, but most often it gets its meals by bullying a pelican or booby to give up its freshly caught fish. The man-o'-war hovers above a flock of fishing boobies, watching as they dive into the sea. When a booby returns with a good-sized fish in its beak, the man-o'-war power-dives recklessly right at the booby. The bird sees it coming and tries to sideslip out of its way, but the maneuver doesn't work. The man-o'-war is too skillful and fast for the heavier, slower-flying booby, and it piles into the booby headlong, scaring it so badly that it opens its mouth to scream and drops its fish. Instantly the man-o'-war flips around the booby, grabs the falling fish, and flees before the booby can even change its course. The whole process is such a skillful robbery that you stand with mouth hanging open in awe and admiration for the rascally black demon as you watch its wild, batlike gyrations again and again. The man-o'-war has a heavy, powerful, hooked beak. He's been known to even break or seriously injure a booby's leg while coaxing it to let go of its catch.

Though the man-o'-war looks all black in the air, at close hand in the sun its feathers glisten with iridescent green and gold. Those on the necks of the males are long and curved, coming to a long, thin point just like the feathers on the neck of a Banty rooster. Females (depending upon the species) have white breast feathers. Two species, the magnificent and the great frigate birds, nest here on Tower. One is larger and a little less gaudily marked than the other. Otherwise they are much alike, especially in their life-styles.

The remarkable bird's most astonishing feature is the giant throat pouch or sac in the male birds. The sac is most evident during the breeding-nesting season, which may be any time for any particular pair of birds. It also may occur every other year. In spite of the bird's clever aerial maneuvers to obtain food, it really is not successful often enough in getting sufficient food to raise offspring every year. The amount of food definitely limits whether the parents can raise a chick to adulthood. Many almost-grown birds are so weak that when picked up and moved they scarcely have energy enough to scramble back to the nest. One I found, though fully grown in size and weighing less than a pound, was little more than a feather-covered bag of bones. Its shrill squawks had dwindled to weak, snakelike hisses.

The bird pumps air from internal air sacs in the bones and body cavity into the throat sac until it tightly inflates to the size of a cantaloupe. The process takes about twenty minutes. Bright scarlet red in color and specked with dashes of black, the throat sac presents a spectacular appearance. The man-o'-war may use the pouch to assert its right to its own territory. Usually, though, it is for courtship display. The male squats in the top of a low shrub about four feet off the ground, his wings folded with crossed-over tips like a swallow. After inflating the throat sac, he will stretch his wings out sideways, draw back his head, thrust his chest full forward, and vibrate his wings in a frenzy of trembling shakes. At the same time he gargles a loud call that I have termed wullowing. It sounds like the bird is saying, "Wullow, wullow, wullow, wullow," repeated many times. If a female lands nearby, the male gets extremely excited, wullows like mad for a while, then conducts a head wagging and bobbing ceremony with his ladylove.

Now it's time to build the flimsy bush-top nest. The male picks up sticks from the ground while still in flight. He snaps off some twigs from dead tree branches, others he robs from the occupied nests of other man-o'-war birds or from the red-footed booby. While one bird guards the nest and builds it to completion, the other brings in the materials. If they leave the nest unguarded for even a minute, neighboring man-o'-wars will swoop down and snatch away the sticks until nothing remains. In three minutes they may carry off an entire nest.

The bird lays only one egg which takes fifty-five days to incubate. Each parent sets three times during the incubation cycle, which means that each bird's session lasts about nine days. It's no wonder then that they lose about one fifth of their weight during the nesting period.

The newly hatched chick is about as cute as any young animal can be. It looks like a great fluff of white cotton candy with two little black flippers sticking out each side for wings and a pair of large round eyes sitting like a pair of spectacles on either side of a too-large beak. The rate at which the young bird grows depends entirely on the success of its parents in finding enough food. Even after getting all of its adult feathers, the young bird may still hang around its parents for a whole additional year. Young males develop lavender-blue throat sacs.

Scientists have traced the Galápagos man-o'-war's ancestry to the West Indies. Other species occur all over the Pacific, but apparently long ago, shortly after the volcano tops pushed above the level of the ocean, a few man-o'-wars got blown out here from the Caribbean Sea by the southwesterly winds of the rainy season. Wherever they've come from, the Galápagos "black spooks of the sea" are certainly one of the world's most unique creatures.

Sea Lions—Playful Puppies of the Water

The strange noise seemed to come from a group of black lava boulders to my right. At first it seemed like a gurgling of the sea squeezing into and out of some subterranean crack in the boulders below, but the rhythm of the sea is slower than the mutters I'm listening to. I'm on Plaza Island. Carefully I creep around the boulders. There I see, sound asleep with belly up, head thrown back, and flippers straight up in the air, a young male sea lion snoring his lungs out. I laugh out loud. He's so sound asleep he keeps on snoring. It's a wonderful way to totally relax. Sea breezes blow in to keep the flies off, and a warm equatorial sun bounces off the boulder, giving my noisy friend enough shade to slumber in.

The sea lion, so helpless looking and ridiculous on land and so perfectly at home in the sea, is a marvelous animal. His streamlined body wastes no motion in the water. Every small stroke of a flipper gives maximum push through the water. It's almost as if the water flows over the sea lion rather than that the sea lion pushes through it. The round plump body rolls first one side up, then bottom or other side up—it doesn't matter. In a flash he can turn end for end and dart off in the opposite direction. Porpoises come to the surface every once in a while and roll forward with arched bodies, dorsal fin in the air, blowhole opening while they suck in air. But so casual is the sea lion in its maneuverings through the water that you never notice when he gets his breath.

The colony of sea lions on Plaza Island ordinarily has about seventy-five members. Recently, though, some strange disease went rampaging through the colonies all over the islands and wiped out more than half of the total population of at least thirty-five thousand sea lions. Experts dissected dead carcasses and tested the tissues in laboratories to see what caused the sudden death. Apparently it was an encephalitis-like disease affecting the animals' nervous systems. Whatever it was, it cut the colony I studied down to about thirty animals. We've seen carcasses of dead sea lions lying up in the bushes at the beach edge all through the islands. Lava lizards gather around the bodies in large numbers, staking out their territories on the carcass and feeding on the flies attracted in hordes to the decaying animals. It will be a half-dozen years at least before the colonies build up to their former size.

The black lava rocks here along the shore at the center of the colony are polished smooth and coated with a white residue that glistens in the sunlight. It comes from the bodies of thousands of sea lions that have dragged their way up from the edge of the water to rest in the shade of the Opuntia cactus trees nearby. The sea-lion colony is rigidly segregated. Just off to the right of my snoozing, snoring friend is the bachelor section. Here young males bark and fuss and push and play together, sometimes on the shore at the edge of the sea, but most often in the shallow water just offshore. The young seal puppies are the most playful of all animals, never seeming to tire of frolicking around with each other—playing tag, follow the leader, chase the sea turtle, or toss the fish. As they grow older, their games become more strenuous. Young males play a sort of "arm wrestle" with their necks. They push against each other as hard as they can press, each trying to outlast the other. It provides good training for the encounters they'll have later on with the old "beach master," or dominant bull of the colony. The young males do not fear people and, in fact, delight in swimming around a human swimmer. They dive under your belly, circle around under you, and pop their heads out of the water just in front of yours as if to say, "What's the matter, you poor fish. Can't you swim any better than that?" Many times after a day on the island we'd come to the shore hot and sweaty. Rather than wait for the dinghy to ferry us out to our small fishing boat, we'd jump into the sea and swim out the half mile or so. As soon as we'd hit the water, so would the nearest sea lion. He'd follow us out, cutting up all the way, then return to the beach in a flash to escort the next swimmer out.

Up the beach from the bachelor bulls lie the mamma sea lions with their nursing pups. They occupy a sort of no-man's-land between the young bulls and the old male and his harem. Each female bears only a single pup who nurses her for fully two years. The pup learns to swim in its first week of life. It can feed itself from the sea but always prefers the company of its mother. When separated, a mother and pup can readily get back together by recognizing each other's voices and by their individual smells. They swim out in search of food only as far as the old bull allows them to. He's not afraid of sharks—in fact, he can send them scurrying by his ferocious attacks. But a lurking shark would like to grab an unwary pup for a quick meal. In contrast to the pup's and the bachelor's relaxed ways of life, the old bull leads a difficult existence.

You can always recognize him by his tremendous size. About seven times heavier than any one of his wives, he may weigh almost a ton. He has an enormous neck and broad muscular shoulders. The top of his head is peculiarly dome shaped. Fights with the young bulls who constantly challenge him for mastery of the harem may have left him covered with scars. At one time he may look after as many as thirty females of all ages. Young males are constantly trying to separate out several of his females or challenge him for leadership of the harem. Usually he wins until old age overtakes him. A younger, more powerful bull may then drive him away.

I watched a big bull with seven cows for most of an afternoon. He spent the entire time circling in the water around and around them. They acted relaxed and unconcerned, but he kept his head high out of the water, barking incessantly, scolding each cow who wandered too far toward the bachelor quarters, nipping her gently, driving her back into the center of his patrol area. Every once in a while he put his head under the water, still barking and scolding. Scientists believe that sea lions can hear each other under the water.

After a while I saw some pups having a great time bodysurfing on the incoming waves. Trying to get some closeup pictures at water level, I scrambled down on a rock that jutted out into the water farther than the others. Intent on getting a good picture, I didn't think about the old bull fifty or sixty feet away behind the outjutting rocks. Suddenly it struck me that he wasn't barking. Uneasily I looked back over my shoulder to where he was supposed to be. At that instant he rose up out of the water onto my rock like some monster from the deep. His mouth opened wide as he uttered guttural snarls. His big canine teeth gleamed at me. Knowing he meant business, I shot off into the water on the other side of the rock. Fortunately he didn't follow, as that would have taken him out of sight of his harem. Instead he just roared a couple of bellows as if to say, "And stay off, fellow, if you know what's good for you!" Local stouthearted Galápagos naturalists claim that all you have to do when a bull sea lion charges is wait until he's a yard or so away, fling up your arms, and shout at him —and he'll stop in his tracks. It takes more nerve than I'll ever have to try it.

The Galápagos sea lions are here by courtesy of the Humboldt Current. Usually they live in the more northern, colder waters. One population of sea lions dwells in the Sea of Japan and another along the coast of California. The Galápagos colony is probably an offshoot of the California group. A few sea lions most likely migrated out here from California just after the ice age when the northern Pacific was considerably colder than it is today. Then as glaciers melted and the seas warmed up, their descendants survived because the cool waters of the Humboldt Current sweep out here from the South American coast, providing the right temperature and supporting a rich fish life. Warm waters to the north and to the south effectively bar their migration in either direction. The sea lions are stuck here and have been so for some time. They have gradually become smaller in size than their California ancestors.

The trained "seals" of the circus are really the highly intelligent sea lion. Most of us have enjoyed seeing them perform and have marveled at their abilities.

The Fly-catching Lava Lizard

On the ground in front of me, lying just where the glaring white beach sand gives way to dense undergrowth of thorny acacia, is a dead sea lion. By the appearance of the taut, sun-cured hide stretched over the fleshless bones, it's been dead for some time. The smell of death is still strong. Hundreds of flies should buzz around the decaying body—but there's not a single one. Do you want to know why? Spaced every six inches or so around the carcass, standing almost vertically with front feet on the body, is a Galápagos lava lizard. I count thirty-four of them. Each poses motionless like some miniature dinosaur statue. Every individual guards its own territory on the dead body. Any fly landing there he instantly catches and devours. The fly doesn't stand a chance of escaping the ring of darting, adhesive tongues. The lava lizards have found the perfect, though to us gruesome, dining table.

They love the sun. All activity necessary for the eight-inch-long reptiles they carry out in the sunny daytime. Their day lasts twelve hours, from sunup to sundown. (Days and nights are equal in length in the Galápagos Islands on the equator.) At night the lizards either bury themselves in loose soil, hide in the ground litter, or wriggle beneath rocks out of sight of the Galápagos owls whose keen eyesight would soon spot a wandering or exposed lava lizard. During the hottest part of the day the lizards like to siesta for a couple of hours—probably because the volcanic rocks and soil simply get too hot and uncomfortable for the little lizards to sit around on rather than for any special need to take a rest.

Besides flies, the lava lizards consume red and black short-horned grasshoppers, beetles, butterflies, and frequently petals and other parts of flowers.

Lava lizards are the most abundant reptile on the islands. Totally fearless of man, they become the playthings of children in the two small towns and five villages scattered through the archipelago. The yard of every house in the town of Puerto Ayora at Academy Bay has its quota of lizards running into and out of the brown-lava-boulder fence surrounding it. Our yard is no exception. It is an almost solid mass of grapefruit-sized rocks. The house sets on a raised-up portion of the yard extending out about six feet all around. The outer yard is two feet lower. The additional wall thus created almost doubles the size of our lava lizard population.

It was a lot of fun to watch the territorial behavior, as the scientists call it, of the attractive little creatures. Both males and females have home territories over which they rule supreme. A male lizard's domain is four or five times larger than a female's. Each male area encloses a number of female areas. They form his harem. He can freely go from one female's space to another's within the boundaries of his own territory, but another male will battle him back to his own kingdom if he ever leaves it. Ordinarily, males will defend only against other males, and females against other females.

The male lizards establish the invisible boundaries of their home areas by repelling any trespassing lava lizard in a most unusual way. The male lizard sidles with his head toward the other's tail. Each animal extends his dewlap or throat flap as far as possible, at the same time flattening his body sideways. Then he stands as high on his spindly legs as he can and raises the crest of scales down the middle of his back. Now the two are ready for battle. To us they look funny—each trying to outbully the other before they ever touch each other. The trespasser may now suddenly lose interest in the whole thing and dart quickly back into his own territory, or if he really thinks the area is his, he'll stand and fight.

First one lizard will suddenly twitch the base of

his tail sideways so that he bops the other reptile in the head, then the second animal does the same thing to him. The engagement is no longer bluff and scare. Just one tail-base blow is hard enough to jar the other lizard, sometimes sending him rolling over and over. I have seen a pair of male lava lizards fight so hard that one batted the other through the air a distance of at least a foot. Each lizard may open his mouth wide at the other but never seems to actually bite. It's a good thing, because their little pointed conical teeth could punch holes in each other. When one lizard finally zaps the other into permanent retreat, he demonstrates his win by climbing up on the nearest rock and doing a series of fast push-ups.

Both males and females use push-ups to show alarm when anything unusual happens. It's very easy to catch a lava lizard by slipping a little string noose hanging from a slender stick or a fishing rod over the lizard's head when it's doing them. In fact, you could probably catch lizards where you live in the same way.

Male lava lizards court females by going through almost exactly the same kind of ritual as when they fight for territory. However they stop short of battling with their tails. If that did happen, the females would get the worst of it because they're only about a third the weight and half the size. Females usually have plainer markings than the males except for a pretty bright-orange to dark-red throat patch or bib. It is unusual in lizards since the males usually have the brighter colors.

Lava lizards hatch from eggs laid over a long

period of several months in shallow burrows scooped out of the soil. The eggs take a long time to develop—two or three months. Each little lizard leads a secretive life after hatching. Too many birds and the Galápagos snake would like to eat it.

The lava lizards of Galápagos impressed Charles Darwin greatly because of their differences in appearance from island to island—a fact which apparently influenced him in developing his ideas about evolution. Of the seven species scattered throughout the islands, each one has its own size, color pattern, and slightly different way of fighting and courting. The biggest—ten inches long—live on Hood; the smallest—five inches—on Charles. A male on Santa Cruz Island is grayish brown in color with black bands lengthwise down his body. His throat is black. The Hood Island male is greenish brown, dotted with black spots. Santa Cruz Island females have a brownish body with red cheeks fading into pink on the neck, while the Hood Island female has a lighter brown body and deep red cheeks and neck.

All of this sounds too technical, but to Darwin—and to you and me—it is extremely important. Either Darwin's idea that all animals have come from a first original form of life is correct, or the Bible story that God created the basic kinds of animals during creation week is true. Both cannot be right. What do the Galápagos lava lizards have to contribute to the two ideas? Darwin thought they represented newly evolving species developing by themselves without the help of God. In other words, "evolution was occurring." True, new varieties of lizards are originating on the different islands, each with its own special characteristics. But when you compare each with its nearest relatives on the South American mainland, obviously it is still basically the same creature. We can see new variations of many animals and plants appearing in nature and, with the help of man, also on the agricultural experiment farms, but most of God's original created types still exist. *No new types have evolved.* So Darwin jumped to the wrong conclusions. His ideas caused thousands upon thousands of persons to reject God and His Word. But nature rightly studied leads us to God, not away from Him.

Turtle Giants of Galápagos

It was a long way to come to see a turtle. But they are not ordinary run-of-the-mill ones. Rather, they are the most famous turtles in the world. I am standing in what is certainly one of the loneliest spots anywhere—the rim of a gigantic volcano in the center of the largest island of the Galápagos Archipelago. Back down the green-carpeted slope and over the greenish rise lies the beautiful blue Pacific—3,700 feet below and 7 miles away. Few living persons have ever come here, but this island is a teeming center of life, for the largest population of Galápagos turtles still living today occupy it. About six thousand of the gentle creatures still hoist their heavy, bony hides up and down the slopes of the island. Three turtles stand within a pebble toss of where I'm sitting watching them and drinking in the majestic grandeur of their hostile yet beautiful environment.

It has been a rugged experience just getting up here. First we came by small fishing boat from Academy Bay on Santa Cruz Island, the site of our laboratory-dormitory building. It took thirteen hours of sailing among the islands to reach Isabela, the largest of all of the islands. Isabela is really just five big volcanoes strung out in an L shape with one small volcano making a hook on the top of the L. Volcano Alcedo has a large crater with a fairly flat floor about half a mile almost straight down from the rim. It is three miles across. The vegetation on the inner wall is dense and difficult to get through. Several big crevices run across the volcano floor. In the distance, several fumaroles mist the sky, and over on the almost bare south wall a semiactive geyser of steam shoots plumes of hot vapor into the air. It reminds us that we are in one of the world's most active volcanic areas. We wonder if we dare venture into the crater.

Our boat had put us ashore in a little cove with a sandy beach, then it went several miles down the coast to a safe anchorage off Punta Alfaro. We hoisted our packs onto our backs and began to climb what looked like an easy several-hour jaunt up the volcano. Unfortunately, the shimmering equatorial sunlight makes distances deceiving. At the end of two hours of hiking up the vast field of whitish, porous pumice, the top looked no closer to us. On and on we plodded into the blackness of a moonless night. The trail virtually vanished as the vegetation at higher elevation became more dense. Zigzag cracks a few inches to several feet wide and inches to five or six feet deep add an additional hazard in the dark. Finally, fearing a broken leg, we stopped for the night. We've come up the gradual slope from the sea. Now we've got to climb the steep part to the rim.

The stars shine in such profusion it seems the heavens will burst for the joy of it. The geometric form of the Southern Cross constellation stands out from the myriad of lesser lights. Off in the distance, wild donkeys bray across the slope to each other. Since the sun disappeared at 6 PM, we have shivered a little bit as the onshore breezes dry our perspiration. For supper we eat a few unroasted peanuts, a piece of dried pineapple, and a fresh orange. We've brought a bare minimum of gear with us, since others warned us of the tough climb. Water is precious. A little brackish seepage from the sea forty miles away on the south end of the island is the only water fit to drink this side of our base camp back on Santa Cruz Island. Already we've discovered that a canteen full of fresh water will not last us the two whole days we expected to stay here. My Clorox-bottle canteen holds a full gallon. That too will soon vanish down parched throats. We roll out our sleeping bags on the ground in a little clearing and soon fall into exhausted sleep, only to scratch ourselves awake a couple of hours later. At first we thought fleas from the wild donkeys had attacked us, but no, turtle ticks cover us. They don't really harm us but keep tickling us as they crawl over our bodies trying to find the best places to begin feeding. It's all but impossible to sleep. Fifty-six ticks later it is daylight. We shiver in the morning cold, eat breakfast, and start up the volcano.

Our sleeping bags we leave spread on the bushes to dry out the heavy night dew. We'll pick them up on the return trip. Shrubs and ferns and mosses now cover the steep part of the volcano. I rest frequently. The slope has now grown so steep it's like going up stairs from clump to clump of grass and shrub. To find footholds we have to scramble back and forth almost as much as we climb. At last we're on top. Our fatigue and soreness we forget at the sight of the spectacular hole stretching out before us. The gigantic pimple of once-boiling rock is nothing when compared to the vast Pacific stretching out to the horizon around the islands. The Pacific is a salty raindrop before the immensity of the heavens over our heads. And the starry universe is but the curved underside of an umbrella when we realize the magnitude of the love of God who called such things into existence for our enjoyment and enlightenment.

Here we see the turtles (usually called tortoises since they dwell on land). As they feed on grass and pay no attention to us, we photograph and watch them go about their business of living just as they've done for the several thousand years the islands have existed. The huge population that once lived all through the islands has almost disappeared. On many of the islands the turtles are extinct. Only a few remain on the others. Four animals survive on Hood Island—one male and three females. The Darwin Research Station personnel are much concerned with trying to preserve the Hood Island species and prevent its extinction. They have taken one male and two females back to Santa Cruz Island, where they keep them in large stone-fenced enclosures to live and lay eggs. The eggs they will artificially incubate, and they will rear the young turtles in pens safe from their enemies in the field. Most of the danger comes from animals that man has introduced into the islands. Wild goats compete for edible grasses, while dogs and rats search out the nests to uproot the eggs and eat them. The latter animals also eat the young turtles while their shells are still soft. Wild donkeys and cattle roll and step on the nests, crushing the eggs.

Man has been the turtle's worst enemy until recent years. During the seventeenth and eighteenth centuries, whalers, sealers, and fishermen all collected the big turtles by the thousands. No reliable figures exist for the two hundred years, but the number of turtles taken was in the many thousands. In the early nineteenth century, records indicate that whaling ships alone took thirteen thousand turtles. Why did they want them? Simple. A full deck of turtles turned upside down—so they couldn't wander around—would live for a long time with no more attention than to have a bucket of seawater thrown on them once a day. On those early sailing vessels it was a common thing to be becalmed without wind in the sails for days at a time. Food and water supplies would dwindle or give out. Then the Galápagos turtle supplied the crew with both. They cooked and ate the turtles' flesh for food and opened their bladders to get about three to five quarts of water from each one. The water was salty tasting and sometimes bitter, but it was better than dying of thirst.

Today the Ecuadorian National Park Service, cooperating with the scientists at the Darwin Research Station, have an active program of research into methods of protecting and preserving the rare and historic beasts. (Historic because Charles Darwin first described them at any length.) All together probably about nine thousand turtles still survive.

The turtles here on Volcano Alcedo have dome-shaped shells, while the ones down on Hood have a high saddlelike arch in front. The necks of the Hood turtles are a lot longer, too, which enables them to browse the cactus pads three or four feet off the ground. Grass is scarce on low-lying Hood, so the animals have especially adapted to survive there. The dome-shaped turtles usually live at higher elevations where the vegetation is lush. All of the turtles consume great quantities of plant material, including flowers, shrubs, Opuntia cacti, cactus fruits, grasses, and herbs. The ones I am watching here on the volcano rim are eating something that resembles chickweed. I pull off some leaves and chew them. They taste about like raw spinach leaves. The turtles' favorite browsing times are early morning and around four and five o'clock in the afternoon. They live a marvelously relaxed existence. Perhaps that is why they can survive to 150 years or more in age—the world's longest-lived animal creatures.

At night the turtles up here wiggle their shells in a rotary motion on the ground to create a depression called a form where they can get their soft parts below ground level. It protects them from mosquitoes and helps to keep their temperature up during the cool of the night. In the turtle preserve on Santa Cruz Island, the big fellows like to get out in a mud wallow and just sink into the ooze until only their shells stick out. Every once in a while the head covered with black mud pokes up for a breath of air. Soaking in the mud bath helps to keep down the numbers of ticks which like to attach to their soft areas.

The mating season occurs during the spring and early summer. The big male beasts pretend to battle by approaching each other and banging their shells together. They try to push and shove each other around, but since all are about the same size and strength, no one wins. Then each male hunts a female to mate with. The males make low rumbling sounds. Such a noise coming from a turtle sounds strange indeed. The female then digs a nest hole in the ground. She never sees the hole since she excavates it with her hind legs. Wetting the ground with urine to soften it up, she clumsily works first one hind leg, then the other, scooping out the dirt. It takes about thirteen hours of hard work before the hole is big enough to satisfy her. After filling it with eggs, she tamps the earth back in, around, and over them. Now exhausted, she finds a shady place to rest for one or two days. In from four to eight months—depending on the number of hot days—the eggs hatch. The little turtles struggle to dig up through the packed, baked earth. Some never make it. The strongest ones manage to pop up out of the ground to begin a life of their own.

A number of birds, such as Darwin's small ground finch, yellow warbler, and beautiful vermilion flycatcher, hop around over the turtles' scaly legs and leg pits, picking off ticks and insects. The turtles show no sign of recognizing that the "cleaners" are around. It's a beautiful symbiotic relationship where both the turtle and the birds benefit. And that is really what nature is all about—everything working together for mutual benefit. Today the presence of sin confuses God's original plan for nature. The law of tooth and claw tries to rule. But examples such as the turtles and the birds show us that it is possible for widely different kinds of creatures to get along together in harmony.

The Powder Puff Bird

Standing perfectly motionless in front of me —one pinkish-orange foot poised in the air as if to take a step the instant I look away—is a lava heron. Its dull gray color blends beautifully with the lava rocks around it. The heron and I have been seeking a place to get into the shade.

Seeing the overhanging ledge of lava rock from up on top of the cliff here along the sea on Hood Island, I searched for a way to climb down without disturbing the nesting boobies and sunning marine iguanas. A wide crevice cutting back into the cliff contained smaller boulders which made a sort of crumbled staircase to clamber down on.

Reaching bottom, I maneuvered back against the cliff base as far from the drenching spray of the rhythmically pounding surf as I could get. As hot as the Galápagos equatorial sun was, I didn't really mind getting wet—I just didn't want to ruin a good camera. I came around a corner to confront my big-footed friend heading for the same shadowy overhang of rocks. It had room for both of us. Since the lava heron was not the slightest bit afraid of me, we both got comfortable at once. I sat on a flat, pitted boulder nicely placed so I could lean back against the cliff. The heron froze motionless, his old-fashioned-shoe-button eyes staring unblinkingly at me as he raised one foot and balanced easily on the other. In comfortable contentment, I sighed. Here was a chance to observe at arm's distance another unique creature of Galápagos.

Lava herons are a species found only in the islands. Other types of little green herons live along water all around the world. Usually they have distinctive color patterns according to the particular species, but the Galápagos bird is a melanistic form. It has transformed its appearance to a uniform dark color as the result of a single change in its inherited characteristics. Scientists call the alteration a mutation. The mutation allows the bird to perfectly blend with its background. When it stands motionless, its outline fades into the rounded curves of the boulders around it. From a distance—though in plain sight—the bird is invisible.

The lava heron's big feet, laughable to look at, are twice as big as they need to be for a bird of its size but are necessary in gripping the curving rocks as the heron leans over the water in off-balance position to snatch small fish for its dinner. The herons don't hesitate to wade into the water after small fish and crabs, but I've watched them mostly walking slowly around small tidal pools. They sneak up on small fish basking close to the surface along the rocky edges.

The lava heron also eats small Sally Lightfoot crabs that accidentally come too close to the bird's spearing beak. The beak is about four inches long, heavy at the base, pointed at the tip. It easily crushes the hard outer skeleton of the crabs to pick out the muscular food inside. If a too-small Galápagos snake comes near the heron, it also gets greedily gobbled down. At night, people have observed lava herons eating insects attracted to the lights of buildings in Puerto Ayora at Academy Bay. A long-necked cousin of the lava heron, a great blue heron in Puerto Ayora, was so tame it came into our kitchen one afternoon and snitched great mouthfuls of freshly cooked rice right out of the pan on the stove. The still-hot rice didn't seem to slow down the big bird's gulping one bit.

While I observe my friend, it watches me. I don't know whether it's a male or a female, since both look alike. But I do notice that its unblinking orange eye has a big, black round pupil. Every once in a while the nictitating membrane or third eyelid sweeps across the eye from side to side like an automatic shutter, keeping the eye moist with body fluids. Since the eyelid is transparent, the bird is able to see continuously, even when it is closed. Its breast has a few streaks of white. In fact, the underparts are all slightly lighter gray in color than the top and wings. The tail is stumpy.

As the heron recognizes that I will not harm it, it relaxes and begins to move around a little. Now it demonstrates why I called it the powder puff bird. On the breast, rump, and tops of the legs of the heron are peculiar patches of feathers. The bird never sheds them when he molts. Instead, they keep on growing. Called powder down, their tips fray and crumble up into a gray, slippery powder whenever the bird rubs its beak over one of the patches.

After the bird has fished for a while, it may have mucus from the fish sticking to the feathers around its head. Other bits and pieces of dirt may stick to the mucus. In other words, the bird just plain gets dirty and needs a bath. It covers the dirty places with powder down. Sometimes its whole head may be dusty white with the powdered feathers. After leaving the powder on for a while to soak up the mucus, the lava heron combs out the dirt and down with the long toenail on each middle toe. Its edges are serrated or notched like the teeth of one of our combs. A vigorous scratching of the dirty feathers with the built-in comb soon gets rid of all the offensive dirt. Now it's time to apply some "hair lotion" to condition the feathers. The heron gently squeezes or rubs the preening gland just above and at the base of the tail to release a natural oil onto the beak. The oil, stroked through all the cleaned feathers, makes them look bright and sleek. Also it waterproofs them so the bird doesn't have to spend time drying out each time it gets soaked by an unexpected high wave breaking on the rocks.

My friend, now all cleaned up and shining, has decided to go out feeding again. Looking up at me, it utters the only song—if by some stretch of the imagination you can call it that—it's capable of—a loud piercing, explosive "skeouw" sound. With that it slowly, majestically, stalks off over the rocks.

The lava heron's courting and nest-building behavior resembles that of the little American green heron. A male chooses a female to impress with a brief, nervous strutting act. Then they begin nest building by constructing a loose platform of sticks in the top of low mangrove bushes at the water's edge. Several birds may nest in the same general area. The female lays three to five greenish eggs which hatch in the short time of seventeen days. Each baby is a ball of fluffy down sticking out in all directions. The young grow fast, gaining nearly a quarter pound a week. In a couple of weeks they're hopping about the bushes into and out of the nest. They use their beaks and feet together to get about. In fact, they're so active they may get too far from the nest and fall down through the branches into the high tidewater and drown.

Since the powder puff birds have no significant enemies, they populate all of the Galápagos main islands and all but the most distant of the smaller ones. It is one species of unique creature whose future doesn't seem to be in danger. The Galápagos heron probably lives as long as its German gray cousin—one of whom reached twenty-four and a half years, a ripe old age for a bird.

Tree Sunflowers

Victor, my rented horse, carries me down through a forest of one of the world's strangest trees. They're tree sunflowers called Scalesias (ska-lee'shuhs). Like many of the plants and animals in the Galápagos Islands, the Scalesias occur only here. No one knows why a daisylike plant actually grows into woody trees here and not in any other place in the world. Probably it results from a series of mutations triggered by something different in the strange volcanic environment.

Ocean and wind currents plus altitude make it possible for plants to grow differently than they do anywhere else in the world. The Humboldt Current comes up the South American coast and swings out to disappear in the central Pacific. The cool waters cause an upwelling from the ocean bottom that makes them rich in nutrients that produce one of the world's richest supplies of fish and a mild climate in the Galápagos. Because of the Humboldt, average air temperature day and night is about 80 degrees. The islands do have two yearly seasons, however. The cool Humboldt causes the *garua* (ga-ru-a) or cool season of the year. Little rain falls then, except for an occasional drizzle in the highlands. It lasts from early summer to the end of the year. At about Christmastime a warm current named after the infant Jesus, *El Niño*, plunges down from Central America and swings out to sea at the equator parallel to the Humboldt Current, then intermingles with it to bring a rainy season in the islands. Beginning in January, it extends through April. Sometimes, though, several years go by and *El Niño* doesn't reach far enough south to supply any rain.

The varying current conditions cause a sort of layer-cake effect of the plant assortments at various altitudes in the islands. The plant groups in turn have influenced what animals live at different levels and on which islands in the archipelago. Boobies and man-o'-war birds are naturally tropical creatures, while the albatross and penguins are normally arctic and subarctic water forms. All live here harmoniously because of the peculiar current conditions.

As I bounce along on Victor down through the Scalesia forest, I think about the different "cake layers" of the island we hiked through yesterday to get up here in this zone of vegetation. The first layer, or Shore Zone, is narrow—only a few yards wide directly on the seaside or along the edge of saltwater lagoons near the shore. The salt water influences the kinds of plants here. Red, black, white, and button mangroves are the main shrubby plant. Saltbush is also common. The first three kinds of mangrove have green glossy leaves while the button variety is more treelike with a brown-ribbed trunk up to twenty-five feet tall. A low-growing fleshy plant with red leaves called Sesuvium covers any bare places where there is a trace of soil. The saltbush is a straggly shrub that will climb the mangroves. It has thick heart-shaped leaves that leave a salty taste when chewed.

The second layer is the Dry or Arid Zone, which rings each island from the shore to five hundred feet up. It's the widest zone of all, covering some of the islands whose volcanic materials rise no higher than five hundred feet. Spiny, thorny plants are most common here. Two of the three kinds of cactus grow into trees. One, the common prickly pear, is everywhere. Another, the candelabra cactus, is less common. It has a large trunk with several vertically ascending ribbed branches bearing purple flowers which open at daybreak. Edible fruits resembling purple plums follow the flowers. The third, more-rare cactus lives on bare lava rock where nothing else will. It looks like a cluster of fat fingers sticking up a foot or so above the rock and covered with a "wool" of inch-long spines which turn black with age.

The most common tree in the Dry Zone is the palo santo, or Holy Ghost tree, easily recognized by its pale trunk, white twisted branches, and broad spreading top. During dry periods it is leafless and dead looking. As soon as rain hits it, small cream-colored flowers appear. Its crushed twigs or leaves have a fragrant smell.

Another shrubby Dry Zone plant is the thorn acacia—a zigzag-stemmed shrub or small tree covered with inch-long paired thorns. A thicket of the stuff is all but impossible to penetrate. It scratches legs and cuts through the thickest pants. I'd rather clamber over rough rocks in the surf along the shore than to try to navigate through an acacia thicket.

The last plant I will mention from this zone is the manzanillo. It's a tree much like an apple tree in size and shape and leaves. It even has a fruit like an apple. Small and yellow, it even smells like an apple—but beware, it's quite poisonous. If eaten, it will cause a blistering rash like poison ivy down the digestive tract.

The third layer from five hundred feet up to thirteen hundred feet is the Transition Zone. The most humid zone, clouds build up in it daily, and heavy fog sits during the *garua* season. It has many species of plants in it. The most common is Scalesia. Mosses, ferns, liverworts, lichens, and vines cover tree trunks and branches. Some of the black species of lichens festoon the trees like ghostly draperies. Patches of guava trees thrive in different places in the islands in this zone. Man introduced them years ago. They provide lots of food for the many wild pigs on some of the islands.

Wild tomatoes bearing small, marble-sized fruits and peppers having tiny bright red fruits grow wild in the zone. The Scalesia trees reach a height of about thirty feet. Many small limbs from a medium-sized trunk bear oval, light-green leaves—mostly in clusters at the ends of the branches. The flowers, about two inches across, resemble shriveled-up white daisies more than they do sunflowers. The wood is soft and the sap gummy. In places it is the only forest tree. Large patches of Scalesia cover acres at a time. From a distance a Scalesia forest appears soft and wavy as you look over the rounded treetops. Riding through the Scalesia forest on horseback requires alertness, or a low branch hooked under your chin will yank you off your mount.

The sunflower family of plants is a huge one with many species. Most of them are "weedy." That means that the wind easily spreads their seeds and they grow well under a wide variety of circumstances. Consequently they are usually the first to appear in a new unvegetated area. The rugged growing conditions in the early days of the volcanic Galápagos Islands strongly affected the ancestors of the Scalesia trees so that a brand-new kind of sunflower family plant has resulted. The marvel of it all is the ability that God first put into all living things back at Creation so that no matter what happens to the environment, as long as a few fundamental substances are present such as water and sunshine, they will survive even though they may have to change their nature drastically to do it. God in His great wisdom thought of every possible future detail in even the life of a sunflower tree.

The fourth "cake" layer is the Miconia Zone. It extends from thirteen hundred feet up to sixteen hundred feet in altitude. Only two of the islands have the zone. Pure stands of the dense shrub Miconia (mi'cone-eea) cover the layer. The shrub grows from six to twelve feet high and bears long, slender, slightly ribbed leaves which look much like those of the cacao plant. Purple berries eventually replace the clusters of small purple-pink flowers. The undergrowth consists of many species of beautiful ferns so thick it forms a carpet underfoot. The dense thickets remind us of the laurel and rhododendron undergrowth in our Appalachian Mountains of the Eastern United States.

If you fight your way up through the Miconia Zone, you suddenly burst out into the open, high-elevation Grassland Zone, which spreads all the way to the tops of the highest peaks. The soil is shallow. Bracken ferns, sedges, and grasses form a low carpet. Frequent drizzles and fogs cover the area. No trees exist here except for a beautiful tree fern that reaches a height of ten feet.

Our island layer cake is now complete. In just a few miles, and in less than 2,000 feet in altitude, we've traveled from the desert, through the tropics, the temperate region, the mountainside, and above the tree line. Each region is different and distinct from comparative ones in other parts of the earth.

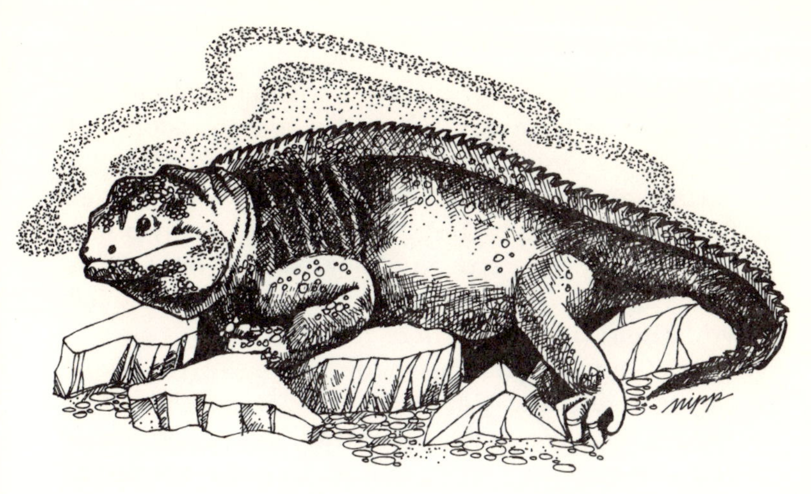

The Galápagos Giant Pale Iguanas

I'm sitting on a lava rock in the heat of the equatorial sun on Barrington Island, watching a male member of one of the world's largest kinds of lizards. Not a big island, it's actually a chunk of weathered volcanic rock about five miles long and several miles wide. It's the only place in the entire world where the big potbellied reptile I'm studying lives. As I look at his pale scaly body and he stares back at me through red unblinking eyes, I, at least, wonder about him.

How is it that he's so different from his cousin on several other of the volcanic piles of rocks nearby? How is it that he's so big compared to his relatives over on the South American mainland, six hundred miles away? How did his ancestors get here? How long has it taken for him to develop the variations that make him a new species that never before existed in history? The answers to my questions do not appear in any book. We can only guess at them. But what about the big lizard? Let me tell you about him and where he lives.

He's resting in the shade of one of the giant cactus trees, and I'm sitting under another. The trees themselves only live in the Galápagos. Their red scaly "bark" looks almost like the trunks of some of the species of pine trees. Spiny oval pads, frequently ringed with pear-shaped fruits or pretty yellow flowers, hang in heavy clusters. The pads grow out from the edges of each other in crooked chains and clumps until they break off and fall from their own weight. The iguanas eat pads, flowers, or fruits—whichever is handiest.

The cactus pad and fruit spines seem not to bother the iguanas at all. The lizard chomps up the whole thing. The spines appear to pass on through the lizard undigested and mostly whole. It would be just as if you swallowed a whole handful of your mother's sewing needles of various sizes. Occasionally a more fussy land iguana carries a spiny cactus "apple" over to a flat rock and rolls it around over the rock with its front foot to break off most of the spines before he eats it. They also eat the flowers of several other shrubby plants.

My nearby friend must weigh about twelve pounds. He certainly looks well fed. A row of scales around his mouth makes his lips look full and puffy. His tongue is pale pink out to the end, where it splits into two pointed red tips. The jowls are fat and loose. When I first sat down nearby, he let me know he didn't like me by ducking his head down and up in several successive jerks, making his jowls shake. Once as he turned his head, he sort of half sneezed and snorted through his nose to further remind me that I disturbed his peace. The iguana's head is double domed in the back part. His neck is thick and bare of spines, but a row of heavy tooth-like spines begins at the base of the neck and runs down the body and out the tail. Some other land iguana must have bitten the end off his tail in a territorial fight, though, for it is quite blunt. Cone-shaped scales, sticking out in orderly diagonal rows like tiny teeth, cover the lizard's legs. Clambering around among the brittle brown volcanic rocks has worn down his black heavy toenails.

The land iguana has no enemies, once it grows up, except for the competition for food from the wild goats. It is good that the Ecuadorian Park Service eliminated all of the island's goats except for two smart old billy goats the hunters can't get near. Now the rare land iguana species has a chance to survive.

My friend has decided to leave me. He scrambles among the rocks, taking long steps and wiggling his body from side to side right to the edge of a two-hundred-foot-high rocky bluff. Over the side he plunges headfirst, his front legs folded back against his body. He lands headfirst in a heap five feet lower down. Carried along by his downward momentum, he goes to the bottom almost as if he were "swimming" on land. His body undulates between the boulders. He finds a shady overhang at the bottom and lies down to rest. I try to think of answers to my questions.

He's so different from his nearest relatives on nearby islands because his ancestors had such hereditary characteristics in their genes when they first came to the island by clinging to some floating tree stump or raft of vegetation. It certainly hasn't taken him millions of years to develop into a new species because even the evolutionary geologist tells us that the Galápagos haven't been here for "millions of years" but only a "few thousand years." Your guess is as good as mine about why the lizards are so much larger than their mainland cousins. No one has a good answer. I see no trouble at all in fitting the development of a new species of lizard into the time period from Noah's flood until now. It is not evolution as generally thought of, but really a pleasant variation on God's original lizard theme.

Silent Flyers of the Night

"Come and see the big cave," one of the students suggested. That was all the invitation I needed. I love to explore caves. The ones I am most familiar with in the mountains west of the Shenandoah Valley in Virginia are solution caves dissolved out of limestone by water. They have stalagmites and stalactites formed slowly from dripping water rich in dissolved calcium carbonate and other minerals. A stalagmite grows up to meet a stalactite hanging down and fuses into a column. At first I wondered if a Galápagos Island cave would have any formations in it, then decided it probably wouldn't since the island contains no limestone, only volcanic pumice and lava rock. We hiked out of town on the only road leading north. It went uphill through pale white, literally leafless, palo santo trees and tall red-trunked Opuntia cactus trees. The ground was red lava rock.

Our guide turned off the road into a thicket. "The entrance is right over here," he pointed. We almost fell into a hole concealed by vegetation, although large enough to drive a tractor-trailer into. Carefully we descended into the cave mouth over pitted lava boulders. In the twilight zone of the cave it was quite cool compared to the temperature above the ground. Our eyes adjusted to the semidarkness. On a ledge directly over our heads sat one of the two species of Galápagos owls. Totally unafraid, it watched us, occasionally blinking one of its large yellow eyes.

The short-eared owl we looked at represented one of the most widespread species of birds on earth. In the northern hemisphere its home circles the globe—continental United States, Canada, England, continental Europe, Russia, Siberia, China, Manchuria, Japan, and Alaska. It also dwells in South America and many of the oceanic islands, including our Galápagos. The barn owl, the other species found here, has an even wider distribution over the earth but is not abundant in Galápagos. The crow-sized, brown-streaked bird above our heads is largely a day-flying owl, preferring either the early morning or early evening hours for getting its food. It seems to like swooping low over the shrubby open country hunting for lava lizards, baby iguanas, rats, and the young of the nesting colonies of birds. In fact, the short-eared owl will sometimes stay in the midst of a colony of nesting boobies for days at a time feeding on the helpless young birds. One owl lived with a colony of swallow-tailed gulls for five days and nights. But the young sea gulls grow fast and soon become too large for the owls to handle.

The short-eared owl, unlike other birds, does not have a definite home range over which it wanders. Instead, the owl covers the entire island on which it lives, searching for food wherever it is most abundant. It's easy to tell the fluffy-feathered bird from the Galápagos hawk when it is in the air by its peculiar way of flying. The hawk soars in circles, glides in long downhill streaks, or flies vigorously in straight fast lines. The short-eared owl, on the other hand, flops around in the air in a slow leisurely fashion resembling more than anything else a huge moth on its erratic journey. Every once in a while the owl utters a sneezy bark that sounds like a shrill "kee-yow."

Our friend on the ledge above our heads has decided to move. He jumps off the ledge and in a silent arc flies up out of the cave entrance to parts unknown. Owls can fly on totally silent wings due to a unique feature not found in other birds. The wings of a hawk the same size, for example, will make quite a whirring sound as the air rushes over the edges of each flight feather. The tiniest parts of most bird feathers are sort of zipped up with tiny hooklets to make of the feather a solid surface against the air. The owl's feathers have no hooklets on their outer margins. Instead, the lead edge of each owl flight feather has little comblike projections that break up the airstream, while the trailing edge of each feather has fringes like a shawl, and the feather's upper surface is downy. Such adaptations all help to muffle the sound of the air as the owl swoops in on its unsuspecting prey.

Here in Galápagos the short-eared owl seems to prefer the open areas of the seacoast and arid zone of the islands rather than the more densely vegetated areas in the uplands. It nests directly on the ground in the open just by tramping down the vegetation and arranging a few sticks around. The female lays from four to seven creamy-white eggs which hatch after a three-week incubation by the female. The young birds will not tolerate a runt in the nest with them. They turn cannibalistic and kill and eat the weaker bird. If it should die by itself, the mother will feed it to the rest of the brood.

The short-eared owl is conspicuously black around the eyes, while the only other Galápagos owl, the barn owl, has white around its eyes. In fact, its whole face resembles a great white heart. People in some localities in the United States call it the monkey-faced owl. Its head is rounded and does not have the little ear tufts of the short-eared. The barn owl, though not often seen, is probably a lot more important as a predator on the rats so abundant in some places in the islands. Scientists have not determined its value in controlling the rat population and thus indirectly helping to maintain the endangered races of Galápagos turtles, but it certainly must be significant. A British ornithologist recorded that a family of seven young owls requires over one hundred rats and other small vermin a day. One half-grown barn owl ate nine mice one after another, though the tail of the last one stuck out of the owl's mouth for some time.

The beautiful rust-colored owl nests at higher elevations in hawks' old nests or on some of the rocky outcrops in the center of the islands. The female lays five to eight or sometimes as many as eleven chalky-white eggs. She begins setting on the eggs as soon as she lays the first one. Thus three weeks later the first one hatches and the rest follow over the next ten days or so. Barn owls mate for life and usually accompany each other on their hunting and exploring forays. They use the same breeding place and nest site year after year.

The bird can sometimes be upsetting to a group camped out at night. Curious, it may fly in to watch what's going on around the campfire. At first it may remain just out of sight while it makes a series of snorelike sounds mixed with hisses, chucklings, and downright eerie screams. Such racket coming out of the night so close by can scare unknowing campers witless. Finally the owl perches only a few feet away to watch the activity. The short-eared owl is equally as curious.

Contrary to folklore, the owl is no wiser a bird than any other. Nevertheless, its forward-peering face, widely rotating head, and secret night ways make it a bird to stir our interest as few others do. The Galápagos owls, though neither rare nor likely to become extinct, are an important part of the islands' natural history.

The Little Penguin People

The swells of the Pacific Ocean rise and fall with the regularity of a heartbeat. Our little dinghy heaves and drops with them. I've come three thousand miles to see the little penguins that live here in Tagus Cove in the Bolivar Channel. Our fishing boat drops anchor in the cove. It has been cramped quarters for the ten members of our expedition. I'll be glad to get ashore for even a few minutes. Boobies and pelicans circle overhead by the hundreds. They're diving into a school of fish. Each bird folds its wings about forty feet up, thrusts its neck forward, and plunges into the water with a splash. Out of sight it goes. Then it pops to the surface, more often than not with a fish crossways in its mouth. Flip! Up goes the fish, tossed into the air to come straight down headfirst into the hungry bird's gullet.

The waters in the cove are cold and clear. We can look over the side of the dinghy taking us to shore and see huge green sea turtles milling around on the white sandy bottom like so many cattle in a pen. The lava rocks along the shore look dangerous with the swells rising so high. One minute we're all set to step ashore on a boulder. The next we're looking up at the rock, for it's now head high. I toss my aluminum Halliburton case ashore and leap after it. Such a case is indispensable. My camera rests safely inside, nestled in foam rubber and insulated from the salt water. After scrambling up the rocks to the top, I turn around to scan the algae-covered rocks emerging from the sea as the tide recedes. According to our captain, the penguins like to pop out of the sea onto the rocks to preen their feathers and sun themselves. I see one and then another. Two of the little "people" in their black-and-white evening dress have just splashed out of the sea. The Galápagos penguin is the smallest species and dwells the farthest north of any of the penguins. Most inhabit the Antarctic, but the Galápagos ones live right here on the equator. I get so excited at seeing them that I almost forget to take pictures. Unfortunately they're too far away, so I circle around the edge of the cove on the bank. Heavy brush and thorns ring the cove, making the going too rough. Turning inland to see if it is easier walking, I step into a clearing under a tree that looks like an apple tree. It even has little green fruits like apples. Then I remember the warning about the manzanillo. Supposedly even rainwater dripping off the tree leaves onto the bare skin will cause a rash like poison ivy. I cut back to the bank closer to the rocks.

Seeing me now, the two penguins become nervous. Of all the Galápagos animals, their kind are probably the least tame. They pick nervously at some algae on the rock with their long, blunt beaks of scalelike plates. When I'm about fifty feet away, they decide I'm too close. Hopping into the water feet first, they disappear. Underwater the penguin is a superb swimmer. It uses its flipperlike wings in short, sharp strokes that cause it to literally "fly" through the water with amazing speed. In fact, the bird catches fish simply by outswimming them. I see my two friends on the surface out in the middle of the cove. They sit deep in the water with only their heads and necks visible. After watching a minute, they vanish altogether.

Later on after dark quite a number of penguins uttered their peculiar "barks" and donkeylike braying sounds from the rocks ringing the cove and along the sides of the channel. The coldness of the water and abundance of sea life makes the area a good place for the penguins to live. The cold Humboldt Current sweeps between Fernandina and Isabela Islands, bringing nutrients up from the bottom, thus greatly multiplying the minute planktonic plants and animals in the surface waters. Small fish thrive on the plankton. Increasingly bigger fish prey on each other up the food chain.

The little penguins construct a simple nest back in a cool shaded cave in the volcanic rock just above the high-tide level. The nest consists of little more than a few stones arranged in a circle on the bare rock. The female lays two eggs some time during the cooler rainy season of the year from May to August. A fluffy brown down covers the infant birds. Both parents feed the baby birds on sort of a regurgitated fish soup, and the nestlings grow fast. Sleek black-and-white dress suits soon replace the down. The young birds quickly learn to swim. With their parents they leave the nest to wander from rocky shore to rocky shore through the islands.

Little Bartolomé Island lies in Sullivan Bay on the east side of Santiago Island. One side of the smaller island has a beautiful little sickle-shaped beach of brick-red sand. At the end of the beach a gigantic pointed rock rises some five hundred feet vertically out of the water like the bow of some giant ship stood on end. At its base cluster smaller rocks and cavelike hollows where penguins like to gather. The water here is quite warm compared to the Bolivar Channel, but the birds don't seem to mind. They appear to come here only after their young are big enough to travel. From the deck of our boat we watch a pair of penguins with a half-grown young one. A penguin emerging out of the water is like a jack-in-the-box. He literally pops straight up out of the water to come down on the rock. The three birds have probably been fishing all day. We see one after another waddle in their stateliest manner to the highest point on their rock.

Their flipper-wings, so effective in the water, look like loose arms on a too-fat body. They stand like three little fat people facing into the setting sun. Their white vests slowly change to shades of pink. As darkness suddenly blots the birds from sight, we hear again their eerie, braying calls echoing over the tropical sea.

We wonder about the Galápagos penguins. Their ancestors probably got carried by the Humboldt Current or some great oceanic storm far out here in the Pacific six hundred miles from land. The Magellan penguins of the South American coast closely resemble them, though somewhat smaller in body size. Estimates of the total number of Galápagos penguins vary from two to four thousand birds, which is not many when compared to some of the penguin colonies of the mainland with nearly a million birds in them. The little penguin people seem to have few enemies, plenty of food, and a good place to live. They probably, therefore, are not in any great danger of extinction like many of the other creatures here.

His Majesty the Galápagos Hawk

Whoosh! That was too close. Up, up he soars, glancing back at me as though to say, "Scared you, didn't I?" He's right—he did. Who wouldn't be frightened to have a winged projectile suddenly come right at your face—feetfirst, talons spread—at a speed of forty miles an hour, veering up at the last second with wings actually touching your head on their downstroke. I stood on a rocky outcrop high up in the middle of Hood Island, out of breath from the climb and sweating from the equatorial heat. Just as I turned around to look over the island from the peak—whoosh. His Majesty the rare Galápagos hawk had dive-bombed me.

The big dark-brown bird swung around about two hundred yards out and aimed for me again. But now I was prepared. He pumped his wings a few times to give initial push to his drive. Then he began his long descent, coming right at me on a straight-line-of-sight run. He looked like a round ball with wings outstretched, tilting down on one side, then the other, to allow for gusty breezes but maintaining his course as straight as an arrow. Even a hundred yards away I could see his yellow feet and legs in the attitude of attack typical of birds of prey. Undisputed king of his mountain, he wasn't about to let anything dethrone him. He let out several piercing cries that carried over the island. I didn't know it at the time, but he was calling his mate, who hunted a half mile or so away. It was awesome to be the target of the totally unafraid and bold bird of prey. I tried to hold motionless and let the big bird zoom by as he had before. At the last instant I ducked, raised my arm for protection, and closed my eyes. The air from his wings brushed my head as he hurtled past. Getting the message, I decided to go down lower among the rocks and leave the lookout point to my aggressive feathered friend.

From the accumulated droppings nearby, it is obvious the hawk has used the point for a long time. After I climb down over the boulders to a lower elevation, the hawk lands above on the perch I just left. His mate joins him. They both call out in loud piercing cries. Although they don't dive again, they watch every move I make. The pair represents one of only about a hundred pairs of

Galápagos hawks still in existence. The bird is another one of those rare endangered species that soon may disappear from the earth. Watching its behavior in its natural habitat is a rare treat.

Every day he sees the primitive beauty and raw nature that I glance over for the first time. I've picked my way through dry grasses, thorny acacia bushes, and gray leafless shrubs to get up here. The island seems hostile to most forms of life. It has no freshwater rivers, streams, springs, or even puddles. Animal life simply does without water except for a light morning dew during part of the year. Rainstorms are nonexistent. Gentle rains may fall every two or three years. The island consists of a giant plate of submarine lava lifted above the ocean. It tilts to form cliffs along the southern coast with a rise toward the center of the island, peaking in the three-hundred-foot-high rocks I'm sitting on. Goats gone wild have heavily damaged the island's vegetation, but game wardens have greatly reduced their numbers in the past few years. It may be too late to save the Hood Island tortoise, since only five survive on the island, and hawks, too, are scarce here. Black-and-red marine iguanas and lots of nesting seabirds live along the coast. Large lava lizards, snakes, Darwin finches, mockingbirds, and Galápagos doves range over most of the island interior. Here, also, exists the only nesting site of the Galápagos albatross. A few cacti and the ever-present palo santo trees add to the vegetation already described.

Off to my left about a mile away I can see Punta Suarez, the westernmost point of the island. Just up the coast from there is the famous blowhole. The incoming surf crashes against the rocks and funnels into a vertical hole, shooting a heavy spray of water high into the air above the cliff like a mighty geyser. Off to the right of the point is the little-sheltered harbor where our two small chartered fishing boats lie at anchor.

The pair of Galápagos hawks have calmed down now and are merely curious about the strange two-legged but wingless creature who has climbed up into their aerie. They jump from shrub top to shrub top, ever closer. Now they approach to within ten feet. Their bright, alert eyes watch every move I make. Their actions show no fear because they have no natural enemies.

Their nest may be somewhere among the big, gray volcanic boulders. Sometimes the birds' nest is in a treetop as a mass of collected twigs. Usually it is simply one to three eggs laid on a flat outcropping of rock. The Galápagos hawk is unique in its family arrangements. One female may have several males helping her to raise the young. Such a family group is most unusual in nature.

Dr. De Vries, director of the Darwin Research Station on Santa Cruz Island, attempted one day to band some newly hatched baby hawks on Barrington Island when one of the parents dived on him with such ferocity that it knocked the helmet off his head. His helpers had to protect him so he could finish his banding job. Such fierceness is also typical of a few of the North American hawks, one of which is closely related to the Galápagos hawk. The dark phase of the Swainson's hawk, a western species, is almost identical to the Galápagos hawk. Both birds have beautiful banded tails. The Swainson's hawks raise their family on the American mainland.

When the adult birds take off from the nest to "hawk," they keep in sight of each other in case one finds food for both. They share whatever food either manages to catch. Since the hawk is at the top of the food chain, it will feed on both carnivorous and vegetarian animals. It eats grasshoppers, marine and land iguanas, centipedes, rats, many species of birds, and even young goats.

As usual, humans had the most responsibility for the decrease in Galápagos hawk numbers. On the large islands, especially where farming took place, hawks would catch chickens. Indignant farmers wiped out the majestic birds with their guns.

On Duncan Island where rats are abundant, hawks, too, are plentiful. But some of the smaller islands now don't have any.

My last encounter with the regal bird occurred on the top rim of Alcedo Volcano, the 3,700-foot-high volcano on Isabela Island. I had just reached the crest with tired back and aching knees and collapsed on the ground in the meager shade of a scrubby palo santo tree. Using my packsack as a pillow, I gazed up into the clear, cloudless morning sky to see not one but fourteen Galápagos hawks hovering four or five feet over me to see if I was something curious to watch or something dead to eat. I lay motionless to see how close they'd come. Three birds landed in the palo santo at my head.

They worked their way down in the tree to within several feet from my face before deciding that I was not yet fit for hawk food.

Later, while traveling around the volcano rim photographing tortoises, the hawks continued to hover nearby to see what was happening. Their gliding command of the air currents coming from the sea up the outer slope of the volcano presented a lesson in aerodynamics. Once again, how the majestic bird fitted into the complicated jigsaw puzzle of life here on the unique islands overwhelmed me. The wisdom of God is manifest in all parts of nature.

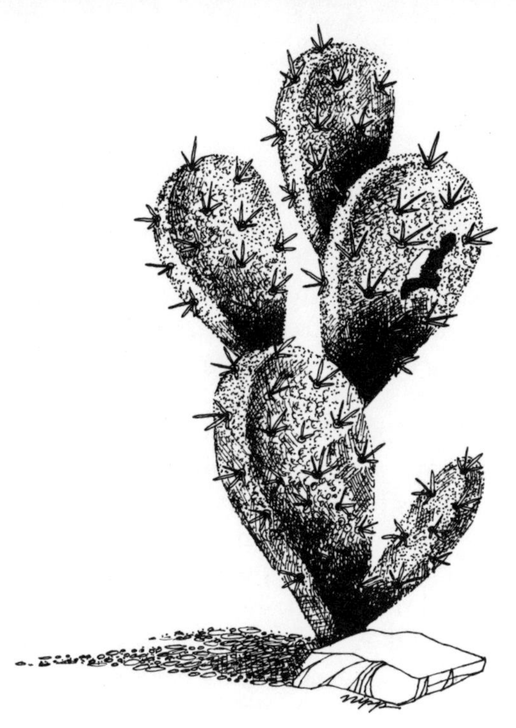

Prickly Pear Cactus

The look of the forest stretched out before me is ghostly. White-barked palo santos intermingle with the red, scaly-barked Opuntia cactus trees. The latter tower over the palo santos. The Opuntia pads—covered with spines, yellow blossoms, and green cactus apples—hang in chainlike clusters from stubby short branches off the main trunks. Younger pads stick up and out in all directions, resembling a tree full of rabbit ears. The blue Pacific beyond forms a fitting backdrop to a scene different from any place else on earth.

I am up on a ridge formed when a big flat chunk of the volcanic island tilted slightly, creating a cliff running from the sea into the volcanic mountain in the center of the island. It's a good place to get a bird's-eye view of the weirdly beautiful forest. So tiny are the leaves on the tips of the twigs, the palo santos appear leafless and bare. It is nature's way of preventing the trees from drying out too fast in the hot equatorial sun.

The Opuntias, up to forty feet tall, exist as trees only here in Galápagos. In the Americas, Opuntia is a widespread species of sprawly cactus that forms dense beds of spiny pads impossible to walk through. One kind of prickly pear extends from the Maine coast to Florida and inland as far as Kentucky. California has 90 of the 250 or more different kinds of Opuntia. Each island in the archipelago has its own combination of one or two of the six species of the arid land plant. The trees are tallest and thickest right here before me on Santa Cruz Island.

It is just a little bit past noon and extremely hot. I sit down on a boulder pocked with pencil-sized holes and lean back against the trunk of a cactus tree after first checking to see that no stray three-inch spines stick out of the bark. Heat waves dance over the treetops. Inky-black Darwin's cactus ground finches flit from tree to tree. They feed on the nectar and soft fruits of the Opuntia. Other birds search for insects on the ground and in low scrub under the trees.

Right near the base of the cliff a crack four or five feet wide opens deep into the earth. Brackish seepage water forms a pool at the always-shaded bottom about forty feet down. A steady stream of finches, doves, yellow warblers, and mockingbirds rise and fall on gentle wings from the water level to the surface. Each seeks the most precious of all of the island's natural resources—fresh water. I have already sampled it. It tastes about like a glass of water would if you put one third of a teaspoon of salt in it. Horrible stuff, but necessary for life if you have nothing else.

The Darwin Research Station has five or six thousand gallons of water in big storage tanks near each of their main buildings. The tanks fill every two to four years when a good rain falls. An American hotel operator also has cisterns to catch rainwater. Together they comprise the only freshwater supplies in any quantity here on Santa Cruz Island. Others may collect a barrel or two, but it is soon gone. Chatham Island boasts the only permanent freshwater stream in all the Galápagos. Right now a swallow of fresh water from my Clorox-bottle canteen filled at the Darwin Station sure tastes good.

The Opuntias, like all members of the cactus family, have no leaves as we ordinarily think of them. The leaflike broad pads are really stems modified as leaves. The leaves of a cactus are its spines. In the case of Opuntia a tiny conelike fleshy leaf emerges once a year in each cluster of spines and falls off. The Opuntia's pads are about a foot long and half a foot wide on the average. Three or four usually hang from each other in a string, or several may dangle together from a single pad to make a cluster. As a cluster grows, it gets heavier and heavier until a slight breeze will cause it to break off and go crashing to the ground where Galápagos tortoises and land iguanas can feed on them. The "skin" of each pad is thick, forming a protective coat to keep it from drying out. Even in the driest climate the Opuntia manages to remain juicy from stored moisture in the leaf.

The Galápagos Opuntias are probably descendants of Opuntias living in the interior of Ecuador. Chunks of cacti probably floated out here soon after the islands formed. The Humboldt Current sweeps up the western coast of South America and out to sea at the equator. Isolated on each island, the original specimens of the same parent stock have gradually changed from each other. The tortoises may have influenced part of the alteration in characteristics.

On four of the small islands up north of the larger ones, the prickly pear is a vigorous, low-spreading species with soft, flexible spines. Each cactus starts out as an erect tree until the fast-growing pads make it top-heavy, and it tips over to develop as a prostrate shrub. Several trunks will grow from the same root. No giant tortoises have ever been seen on these four islands. On the other islands, the Opuntia may have at first matured in a similar way, but continuous feeding by the tortoises would tend to wipe out the lower-growing cacti. The taller ones would survive better.

On Hood Island the tortoise changed along with the cactus. The island's turtles have high saddlelike shells, narrow and flared outward and upward in front. They also have long necks and legs which enable them to reach the drooping branches of the cactus. Here the tortoise must be able to stretch up to eat, or it would soon die out, as ground vegetation suitable for food is practically nonexistent. On the other islands the tortoises have dome-shaped shells and their necks and legs are not so long. They have lots of grass and low shrubs to feed on except during the dry season when they consume the fallen pads of the Opuntia and do not have to stretch.

The young Opuntias are literally solid masses of hard, long spines, which make it impossible for the tortoise to eat them. Rapid growth in height soon puts the pads out of tortoise reach. As the trunks thicken, the spines fall off, and a smooth, paperlike red bark replaces them. Spine scars punctuate it. The trunk never is really woody but just tough fibers. Goats sometimes chew clear through a trunk like a beaver in order to get at the pads and fruits at the top.

Opuntia fruits are at first green, then they change to red as they ripen and fall. The fruits are sweet and a little fibrous. Both tortoises and land iguanas love them. The large, spiny seeds don't seem to bother the tortoise at all. In fact, they will pass right through the tortoise undigested. In the fecal ball the seeds have a ready-made supply of nutrients to get them started during their early, critical growth period. A tortoise wandering around from place to place acts as a natural distributor of the seeds.

Goats on several of the islands have replaced the tortoise as the primary cactus eaters. Ecuadorian Forest Service wardens are now working at exterminating the goats from the islands. Not only will that make it easier for the tortoises to survive, but it also will give the Opuntia a chance to reestablish itself in places where goat foraging has heavily damaged it.

The Galápagos tree cactus is one of the world's more interesting plants. It appears that a primary power God has put in both plants and animals is the ability to adapt to meet the rigors of environments even as arid and rugged as that of Galápagos.

Bobo the Clown Bird

It's a perfect day. The deep blue tropical sky has a few fluffy clouds scattered around. The Pacific Ocean here in the Bolivar Strait between Narborough and Fernandina Islands is crystal clear and cold. From the deck of our little fishing boat I can look down through fifty feet of water and see giant green sea turtles shuffling around on the white bottom like big brown paving stones with legs. A ten-foot-long shark passes lazily under the boat. Of all nature's creatures, it is the most dangerous because it is so totally unpredictable. A school of small fish churn up the sea surface in a two-acre patch nearby. A school of larger fish feed on them from beneath. The little ones jump clear out of the water, trying to escape. The boobies and pelicans have spotted the leaping fish and dive from above.

The masked boobies especially plunge spectacularly into the sea. They wheel and arc above the mass of seething fish, their goose-sized bodies supported by six feet of outstretched wings. Seeming to pause in midflight, they hover an instant, close their wings only slightly, plummet straight down fifty or sixty feet, and like a spear cleave the water with only a little splash. The booby goes under the water several feet, arches its body upward, and grabs the fish on the rise—usually swallowing it before surfacing. Everything takes place in one smooth, fluid action. An extensive network of air sacs under the skin helps to cushion the bird's crash into the water and also determines the depth of its dive.

Hundreds of masked boobies attack the school of fish. Each one looks as though it's diving faster than the one before it. It's breathtaking to watch. The white bodies and coal-black wings and tail stand out against the blue-sea background. Some blue-footed boobies are here too. Less-spectacular looking, they make up for it by diving in unison. A dozen blue-foots at a time will suddenly upend and head toward the sea—all in the group at precisely the same angle. Scientists believe that one bird whistles to signal the moment to dive.

Hovering above the diving boobies like black imps are the man-o'-wars, watching for the unlucky booby who comes up into the air with his newly caught fish. Instantly the man-o'-war dive-bombs the booby and scares him into dropping the fish. Then the man-o'-war, who never dives into the sea himself, snatches it out of the air. Sometimes a man-o'-war will terrify a booby by grabbing it by the tail. The poor victim squawks in fear and drops his fish.

The name *booby* comes from the Spanish *bobo,* which means clown or dunce. Early Spanish explorers thought the showy birds were stupid because they allowed the sailors to walk right up to them. Sometimes boobies would land on a sailing ship's rail and sit there quietly while a hungry sailor would slip stealthily up and grab the bird.

Bobo is a gentle bird but not stupid. It is simply a large seabird that for some reason has never developed much fear of man. Seen up close, the booby has a black face mask surrounding piercing orange eyes under overhanging white eyebrows. His sturdy large bill is tinted yellow-orange in color.

Sailors have watched boobies swing back and forth across the bow of their ship, keeping a close eye on the foremost edge of the bow as it cleaves the water. Flying fish disturbed by the ship leap out of the water to glide twenty or thirty feet through the air. The booby, carefully gauging the fish's angle and speed of flight, will dive on a slant to intercept the fish just before it hits the water. The action is similar to that of the cowbirds and cattle egrets who follow after a herd of cattle, eating the insects set to flight by the walking animals. Flying fish seem to be the main kind of fish consumed by the masked booby.

Ornithologist Robert Cushman Murphy walked

up to a nesting booby on La Plata Island in the Pacific, and it disgorged seven flying fish, each seven to ten inches long. Dr. Murphy's guide, the lighthouse keeper on the island, promptly picked up the fish to use them for bait. He told Dr. Murphy that he and his son got all of their bait by walking around through the bird colony and tickling the throats of the birds with a little switch to make them give up their freshly caught meals. It is no accident that the range of the booby around the Pacific Ocean coincides with that of the flying fish. Like all other fish-eating seabirds, though, boobies will not turn down any other kind of fish they can catch.

Bobo is the most common seabird in the Galápagos Islands. He exists in colonies of large numbers on some of the rocky cliffs high above the sea. If you saw any one of the three kinds of boobies found there, you'd think it was just like the mainland South American boobies. The expert, however, can see little differences that cause him to classify the birds as different subspecies. The subtle variations will become more distinct as time goes on because the birds have made a good life for themselves here and no longer intermix with the populations on other islands or on the mainland. Some of the changes will have little effect on the birds' lives, but others will make it easier for the birds to live here. The process of gradually becoming more and more different from the species' nearest relatives we call microevolution. It happens wherever a group of plants or animals get separated from the main population of that organism —almost as though our Creator knew that some kinds of living things would fall on hard times in their lives, so He made them in such a way that they could develop changes that would make it easier for them to survive in the new environment. If He hadn't done so, many parts of the earth would have nothing living on them, nor would our planet have nearly as many animals and plant species as we see today.

Microevolution is far different from the main theory of evolution. Scientists who believe in the latter, and most of them do, assume that if enough time goes by, not only will new species develop, but so will new larger categories of living things. To put it another way, the evolutionist holds that if every organism that ever lived were alive today, he could arrange them so it would be possible to trace the ancestry of any two groups—whether they be ferns and starfish, or boobies and land iguanas—back to a place where they had the same ancestor.

Darwin looked at the animals and plants here in Galápagos and decided that he was seeing evolution in action. He drew large sweeping conclusions from the microevolution he observed here, and as a result, millions of people have turned away from the Creator-God of nature ever since.

However, as I stand on a cliff on Plaza Island with nesting masked boobies all around me—the males making funny little whistling noises and the females yakking it up with trumpetlike calls—my faith in God grows stronger. The operation of blind chance simply cannot account for the marvelous design and beauty that I see in the birds before me.

Blue-footed boobies are scattered here and there

among the masked boobies. Their body colors are not as pretty as the masked boobies', but their bright blue feet and legs certainly stand out in sharp contrast to their gray-black rocky surroundings. They raise two or three young ones a year to only one each for the red-footed and masked boobies. Also the blue-footed can feed closer in to shore than the others because of its ability to dive into shallow water. A bird diving down from fifty feet will bob up like a cork from water only two feet deep.

The red-footed booby is the smallest of the three kinds and also the most different in its way of life. It nests in trees. On Tower Island 140,000 pairs of red-foots inhabit the plateau above the sea. The nest is a bunch of sticks just piled up without much care in the outer branches of the palo santo trees. Seven or eight pairs of birds may share the same tree. While one bird sits on the single egg, the other perches on a limb nearby. The red-foot's feet are adapted to grasp the limb and hold on. A masked booby placed on a limb, however, will fall off. The male red-foot vigorously protects an area out to about six feet all around the nest. When I walked up close to a red-foot's nest, the male stood up as tall as possible, flapped his wings, and screamed fearsomely at me. Needless to say I didn't try to touch him. I didn't want that strong, spearlike beak to stab me.

The masked booby nests on little ledges anywhere they stick out of the cliff along the ocean's edge. The nest rests directly on the ground among small pebbles. Two eggs laid five days apart hatch, but only one chick grows up. Apparently the parents only bring in enough food to raise one bird—the bigger, more aggressive one. The other one starves to death. Nature's ways in a sin-damaged world are harsh.

Most nesting birds have brood patches, or bare places on their breasts, where all of the feathers have fallen out so that they can hold their warm bodies directly against the eggs to incubate them. The masked booby has no brood patches. Instead it has big feet with webs between all four toes instead of just between three toes as in other seabirds. Each foot has a good supply of blood vessels so the bird incubates its eggs under its feet instead of against its body.

The young bird sticks its head down its parent's throat and feeds directly on food in its crop. If the fledgling should wobble on its weak legs only six feet away from the nest, the parents seem unable to find it. They'll continually search the bare ground where they are nesting. No matter how much the little bird peeps and hollers and though in plain sight, it will starve to death unless it can stumble back to the nest.

Such strange bird behavior puzzles us. Without knowing more about the boobies, we can only guess why they are the way they are. Man alone, as an adult, needs no instincts to help him survive in a hostile world. God has given him not only the ability to think but also the ability to act on his thoughts.

The Galápagos Flightless Cormorant

When you first see a Galápagos flightless cormorant standing on the rocks five or six feet from the sea edge with its wings outstretched, drying in the sun, you feel sorry for it. Its few scraggly wing feathers somehow look especially pathetic. Imagine a blackish-brown bird with a duck-sized body, a neck half as long and as graceful as a swan's, and wings that look normal folded on the bird's body but when extended make the cormorant look as though it just escaped from a cat. Fortunately you don't have to worry about the unique bird, for it is one of the best fish-catchers in all the sea.

The flightless cormorant lives only in three

small areas here in the islands—along the coast on each side of the Bolivar Strait, and on the west coast of Isabela Island. They are places where the water is coldest and the fish most abundant. The water here is fairly shallow and the sea bottom is rocky, affording lots of places in which fish can hide. Flat rocks sheltered from the wind and rough seas at the ocean's edge make good places for the cormorants to come up out of the water. The cormorant can't pop up out of the water like a penguin when it comes ashore. Instead, it clambers to land on the crest of a wave. So with plenty of food and no enemies, the cormorant faces no danger of extinction. Only about one thousand of the birds exist, which makes them one of the world's rare species.

The big flat rock I'm crouching on is covered with white guano accumulated from years of occupation as the nesting site of the flightless cormorant. The sun reflects brightly back into my eyes. It doesn't seem to bother the nesting cormorants beside me at all. The rock contains six nests, each with its pair of birds. I've been slowly moving closer and closer to one nest. The male on it protects two wobbly birds that just hatched earlier in the morning. Every once in a while one sticks its black head out from under its father's body. Down covers it like a baby chick. The father makes noises that sound like static on an old worn-out radio. I'm only a foot away from him. He doesn't seem too upset about my proximity. Like nearly all Galápagos animals, the flightless cormorant has no fear of man.

When I came by here yesterday, I gently lifted

the setting bird up off the nest to see what the eggs look like. Each one had a bluish-green shell with a few blotches of white limy deposit on it. Sometimes the nest may hold three eggs, and though all may hatch, usually only one bird survives to adulthood. The parents take turns covering and guarding the chicks. Each time the male comes in from the sea he brings his wife a mouthful of dangling brown algae. She takes it from him and fits it around the outside edge of the nest. The cormorant constructs the nest, about two feet in diameter, from the algae, a few sticks, various bones of dead fish, and a dried-up starfish or two. On the inside they cover it with a layer of down feathers from the adult birds. Few seabirds in the tropics bother to use feathers in their nests. The cormorant's body feathers are really more like soft dense hair, something like a penguin's feathers. They give the body an almost mammal-like appearance, and when built into the wall of the nest, they provide a windbreak and screen to protect the infant birds. The whole nest stands about a foot high. The same pair uses it year after year.

The just-returned male, after emerging out of the water, stands with body upright and wings outstretched, drying for twenty minutes or so. Then he waddles slowly over to the nest, rolling his streamlined body from side to side. At the nest he raises and lowers his head while gently pushing against the female. She bobs her head several times in recognition as if to say, "Okay, just a minute, Pop. Don't be in such a hurry. I'm leaving." Then she goes to hunt food herself.

The cormorant's feet are placed so far back on its body that it has to stand upright in order to balance and walk at all on land. In the water all awkwardness disappears; the cormorant is now a highly efficient swimming machine with his webbed feet pushing him along at great speed. Since his wing and contour feathers are not waterproofed with oil like most seabirds, he gets water-soaked and sits low in the water with only head and neck sticking out. Water fails to penetrate the dense body feathers though. They also hold in the bird's body heat in the cold Galápagos waters. The cormorant does not use his wings either in the water or on the land. He behaves more like a submarine than a bird anyway. Floating on the water, he raises his periscopelike neck and turns his head each way, looking over the situation before upending and diving. The bird may travel over a hundred yards underwater before surfacing again.

I watch the female here waddle over the ground, occasionally hopping with both feet together across a narrow crevice in the lava rock. She pauses at the water's edge for three to four minutes before jumping in. It looks almost as though she gave herself a pep talk to go ahead and get wet. She lowers head and body and slides forward into the sea with no splash. After swimming out about ten feet, she glances all around, then curves forward into a perfect dive. I wait for her to come up, but never do I see her surface. Her mate in the meantime croaks harshly at me as he protects the nestlings. The bright sun sparkles back at me from his glittering bright blue eyes. The black pupil is a tiny pinhead speck. His beak is open and his throat pouch vibrates much the way a dog pants. The cormorant pouch is like a pelican's but not as large. The flightless cormorant can feed on large fish and even octopuses due to its large, strong beak. A downcurved hook at the end makes it easy for the bird to grab a big eel or octopus in its rocky undersea hideaway and snatch it out to swallow it whole. At a single feeding a flightless cormorant can consume two dozen seven-inch-long herring. That's a man-sized meal for an adult human. One cormorant swallowed a fourteen-inch eel.

When one of the parent birds returns from a fishing trip, the young bird (only one survives after about the third week) gets highly excited. It pokes and nips at its parent's throat, begging for something to eat. The adult, however, just ignores its pleas for an hour or two. Scientists believe that such behavior may fool the frigate birds who might otherwise attack the exposed cormorant, knowing that it has just arrived from a feeding trip. Anyhow, the flightless cormorant never has to go through the humiliation of losing its meal to the frigate bird, as do its hapless associates, the boobies. Finally the parent bends down over the chick and regurgitates food into the chick's open beak.

Cormorant courtship is gentle and graceful in its movements. It begins at sea with an aquatic dance. The two birds swim around side by side, their necks arched in graceful, swanlike curves. Each holds its neck against the other's. First one, then the other, lifts its head and shakes it while making a growlinglike call by sucking in air. Both birds will rise half out of the water, point their heads and beaks skyward, and after flapping their wings and shaking their bodies vigorously, head for land. The male presents his prospective mate with a beakful of seaweed. She takes it to the nest, where she drops it, to use later in repairing the nest. The male may pick up the seaweed again and again, offering it to the female. Each time with great patience she accepts the gift and places it near the nest.

Courtship ends when the female climbs on the nest and begins to work the little pieces of algae around the outside into the nest wall. The male brings her more until finally she is satisfied. She now settles down to the task of egg-laying while her mate remains close by, preening his feathers or standing asleep balanced on one foot with head folded against his back.

The nesting area I'm watching is isolated from the big colonies of other seabirds along the cliff. The only other creatures associating with the nesting cormorants are the lava lizards that dart in to catch flies attracted to a dead baby bird. Occasionally a marine iguana walks slowly through the nesting area. Neither bird nor lizard pays any attention to each other.

The strange and marvelous birds were unknown to science until 1900. Now having read this chapter, you are just about as much of an expert on the life of the flightless cormorant as any scientist, for what I have told you is about all that we know about them. They represent a real genetic triumph —rarely does change in heredity take an animal out of the air and fit it so perfectly for the sea.

The Galápagos Pelican

The big brown bird was in bad shape. Because it was weak from hunger, we could easily pick up the pelican. Being just skin and bones, he voiced no more than a gentle hiss of protest. Examining a piece of wire that appeared stuck in his throat pouch, we discovered the reason for his fast. Somehow the pathetic Galápagos pelican had ripped its pouch from throat to bill tip. Each time the bird caught a fish in its throat pouch, the fish fell through and escaped. Someone had tried to help the pelican by wiring the two halves together with a piece of heavy wire, but the fish still slipped through. With a finer wire we stitched the two pieces of flappy flesh together their full length and turned the great bird loose. The pouch would never grow back together, but at least the bird could eat again.

Pelicans are a favorite bird for postcard pictures around the world. They somehow manage to make you smile or just downright laugh out loud when you see them. The bird has a large ungainly body, big webbed feet, a round head, and that long, too large beak with its huge sagging pouch. Even more humorous is it to watch their stately manners when they walk around on land. Their dignified, pompous behavior with head erect and beak tucked into the neck doesn't match their ungainly appearance. Whatever you think about a pelican on land, however, your smiles turn to looks of awe and admiration when you watch one in the air. The Galápagos pelican, though smallest of its species, is the largest bird in the islands.

A five-foot span from beak to tip of tail and seven-foot wings class the pelican among the world's largest birds. Both the Old World and the New World have representatives of the ugly but interesting creatures. Florida has a sanctuary on Pelican Island where some two thousand birds live. The Galápagos birds are close relatives of the American brown pelican. Each bird is white on the top and sides of the head and chestnut down the back of the neck. A white line runs down each side of the neck. The body is brown, the feet black, and the wings a dull gray.

We'd better enjoy pelicans while we can, because they are dying out. Pelican eggs have such soft, thin shells that their parents squash them under their feet before they have a chance to hatch. DDT accumulating in the sea causes it. Rain washes the widely used chemical for killing insect pests from the farms of America into the ocean. There the plankton (minute animals and plants) take it up. Plankton-eating fish collect the DDT ten times more strongly in their bodies. Larger fish eating the smaller ones concentrate the DDT another ten times. Pelicans eating the larger fish again increase the DDT ten times. Now the amount of the deadly chemical has risen to a thousand times in the pelicans' bodies over that of the plankton, enough to thin their egg shells and cause death to some adult birds. The death and eventual extinction of some species of wild animals are a tough price to pay for controlling insects on our farms, especially when other ways to do it are possible. (Governments ban DDT in many places today.)

Some biologists have predicted the eventual death of all sea life from substances that man has added to his environment. If that actually happens to us, more people will die from starvation caused by losses of food grown in the sea than would be fed by grain protected from insects by DDT.

Pelicans in general have gotten used to man and are accustomed to hanging around harbor areas. Here they beg food from fishermen cleaning their catch for the day. A fish head thrown up among a flock of the hovering birds causes great excitement as they all dive for it at once. It's a brilliant exhibition of aerial maneuvering.

The pouch doesn't store food as some think, but

it only catches fish and holds them until the pelican can swallow them. Sometimes the big birds will swim through a school of fish on the surface with their heads lowered into the water, scooping up a pouchful at a time. The pouch holds two gallons, the stomach only a little over two quarts.

Usually the Galápagos pelican glides back and forth about thirty feet above the water, watching for a school of fish just under the surface. Majestic in flight, the pelican wheels and turns in great circular glides. Two or three flaps every once in a while keep the bird at the right altitude. Once he spots a fish, the great bird extends his wings straight backward and dives with beak thrust forward like some knight of old on horseback charging an enemy with his lance. He will sometimes plummet into quite shallow water. The great beak opens and closes on a fish grabbed crossways. The big bird bobs to the surface quickly. A mass of air sacs scattered under the skin and in his bones make the pelican as buoyant as an air-filled balloon. Tilting his bill sideways, he empties water out of the pouch. Then flinging up his great beak, he tosses the fish into the air and catches it headfirst. It goes down with one gulp. Back into the air the pelican wings on its tireless way. Fishing is its major activity, and for good reason. It takes about one hundred and fifty pounds of fish to raise one young pelican to breeding size.

The Galápagos pelican's nest is a great flat platform of sticks on the top of a clump of mangrove trees. The trees, only about ten feet high at the water's edge, are tough and dense. Eight or ten nests may cluster in the same clump of mangrove trees. Each nest will have its usual fat, fast-growing baby bird. The female lays two or three white eggs a little larger than chicken eggs. Most young birds starve because they never learn how to eat.

Strangely, pelican chicks can cry out and grunt while they're still in the egg. When the egg hatches, the chick comes out naked. It uses its wings like a pair of front legs to crawl about the nest as though it were a lizard instead of a bird. In a couple of days a fine coat of yellow down feathers develop. The parent bird regurgitates half-digested fish into its beak and lets the "fish soup" dribble into the chick's mouth. The chick will eat so much at one time that it will lay over on the nest with neck outstretched and only half-conscious. Later on when it gets larger, it may, after feeding, run around the nest and through the treetop as though crazy. It hisses, bites its wings, and swings its head from side to side in a dazed fashion. Sometimes a young bird will get so excited over a particular meal that it falls down through the mangrove tree and hangs itself by its neck in a tree crotch.

In just two months, a young bird can fly. It takes three years, though, before adult plumage replaces all the down feathers. A superstition dating from the Middle Ages claims that pelicans feed their young on their own blood obtained by puncturing their breasts with their beaks. The pelican has also gotten identified with Christ's suffering on the cross. It is a symbol of charity and piety; thus it appeared on the shields and banners of knights and ancient feudal kings.

As I sit here on a gigantic log at the end of the wharf in Puerto Ayora, Academy Bay, I see seven Galápagos pelicans take to the air all at the same instant. Climbing high, they head out to sea on a fishing expedition. Making a single line, each spaced precisely the same distance apart, they cross over the golden orb of the sun sinking into the ocean. To me, the birds represent an order and precision that are characteristic of all God's works—they are "fearfully and wonderfully made."

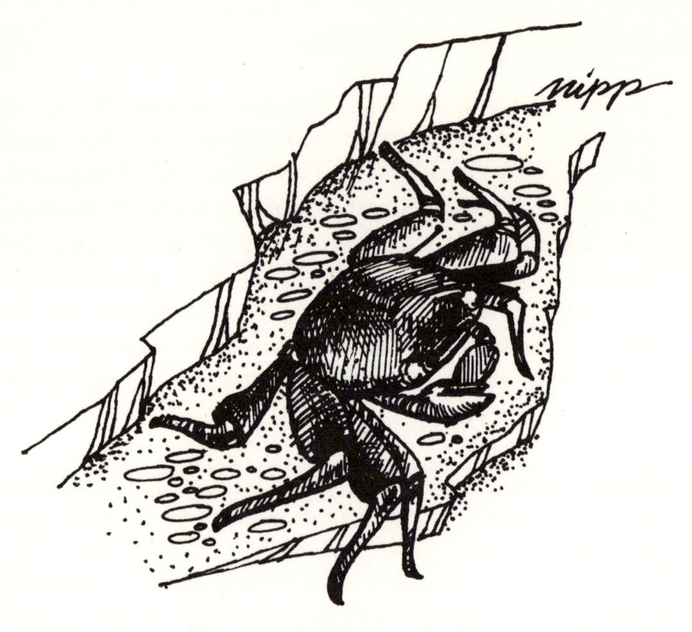

Sally Lightfoot the Crab

How would you like to: swim faster than a mackerel; have a natural coat of armor (no skinned elbows or knees); have a built-in scuba system so you can either breathe in the air or underwater; have eyes on stalks so you can see in every direction except straight down; be able to grow a new arm or leg if the old one gets injured or broken; and, finally, be able to produce five million offspring at one time? Sounds incredible, doesn't it? The Sally Lightfoot crab can do all of those things. Most people don't think of crabs and crayfish as interesting animals—mostly, I suppose, because they never seem to do anything exciting.

Out on Espinosa Point in the Galápagos Islands, thousands of marine iguanas roam the bare black lava rock. Hundreds of bright orange to deep red Sally Lightfoot crabs mingle with them. The crabs, like the lizards, never venture far from the sea. Let's watch one of the crabs for a while.

Here's a big old female. She's a brilliant crimson red. Every detail in her body stands out in bright contrast against the black rock. Why has Nature almost outdone herself in making Sally so conspicuous? After she grows up, she has few enemies on land and is perfectly safe out in the open air on the great boulders by the sea. But why red? Why not dark green, or gray like the iguanas who also have no enemies here in the open, or blue like the famous Chesapeake Bay crab? I don't have an answer but will guess that a crab's colors probably result more from its body chemistry than from the fact that the environment selects certain color genes for some reason of protection.

Consider this: If you drop a mud-brown crayfish into a pot of water and cook it, the animal turns red. So does a lobster when you steam it. Why? Because the acid juices cooked out of the animal react with chemical compounds in the shell to make the bright red color. Also, in West Virginia in the Monongahela National Forest, small streams flow through the limestone rocks. Their water becomes alkaline from dissolved carbonates. The crayfish in the streams are a deep, beautiful blue. The blue crayfish represent a rare species, only a dozen or so having ever been found. The water conditions then must be special. The tropical equatorial sun beaming down on the Sally Lightfoot crabs, which spend 90 percent of their time sunbathing, may over the years affect their shells and be responsible for their red color. Young crabs are more orange than the adults. Each time a molt takes place, the crab is bigger in size and a shade more red.

As I inch closer to her, the female crab stands up on her six walking legs, ready to race over the rock and disappear into an inaccessible crack. For a few feet she runs sideways, then pauses. Her body bobs up and down rhythmically and gracefully as she hurries along. It's more like a dance step than just plain running. Her feet click against the rocks. Carefully and slowly I sit down, wanting to look her over for a few minutes. To her crab mind I'm now a piece of the rock and therefore nothing to fear. Her shell rests on the rock. She angles her big pincers across in front of her, ready to strike out against anything daring to come too near. Even an adult human being like me watches out for her claws. Sally has a formidable strength in her pincers, and she knows how to use them with surprising speed and accuracy.

Motion close at hand sends Sally running. She has a special kind of eye that reacts in the daytime more to motion itself than to what makes it. Each eye is on a stalk about one-half inch long. The stalks are hinged at the bottom so they can fold down into a groove in the shell for protection when Sally is attacked. The brownish compound eye covers the top end of the clublike stalk. Part of the eye extends around behind the stalk as well as over the top, giving Sally excellent vision all the way around.

Her eye consists of 2,500 little square units all arranged in orderly rows. Each little "eye" during the day sees only what is straight out before it. A curtainlike black-pigment cell completely encloses each single eyelet so that no light entering one eyelet can bounce to adjacent ones. As something crosses the crab's view, it excites first one eyelet, then the next, and on and on. The total image forms a mosaic. It is a sensitive "early warning system" for day vision. At night the pigment-cell "curtain" rises out of the way. Light entering an eyelet can also bounce to nearby ones, thus making the whole eye much more sensitive to the weaker illumination of evening and night. Now the mosaic becomes an overlapping continuous image making the whole picture.

Every once in a while Sally tilts her eyestalk partway and rubs one of her long legs over her eye to clean it much the way a windshield wiper works.

Her hard shell contains chitin (kī-tin), a tough, slightly flexible material. It's actually a living plastic. Such things as alcohol, lye, dilute acids, and digestive juices will not dissolve it. In an old crab, the shell is more brittle because it has become impregnated with the chalk chemical calcium carbonate—the same stuff in stalactites in caves. You know how hard they are if you've ever bumped your head on one while exploring. Sally sheds her suit of armor seven times during her first summer—the time when she grows the fastest. Her mother laid between one million and five million eggs. Most of them hatched into little creatures that look for all the world like tiny swimming derby hats with a pair of eyes on the front.

Crab larvae, which scientists call zoeae, comprise a major part of the plankton in the sea. Without plankton we would have no fish or whales. For example, it takes a thousand pounds of plankton to make ten pounds of fish-eating whale or a hundred pounds of great blue whale, which eat plankton direct. In other words, it takes 1,600,000 pounds of plankton to grow one great blue whale. Now you can see the importance of crab larvae in the scheme of the sea. Those that escape being eaten by something grow into a second larval form called a "megalops." The megalops becomes a tiny crab which repeatedly molts until it reaches final adult size. Sally may be the only one of her brood of millions of eggs to become an adult.

The molting process in crabs is quite different from that of insects. Remember that cicada shell you found sticking to a tree trunk in your backyard? Crabs don't leave whole shells. Instead, the cells just under the shell secrete a fluid that softens it up so that enzymes produced by the same layer of cells can digest the old shell. Much of the old shell then goes into making the new one underneath it. When the new one has formed, the crab swallows air and water to swell itself up so that pieces of old shell break up and fall off. The new shell is soft for a few days until the chitin "plastic" sets. The whole process operates under the control of some peculiar nerve cells in the eyestalks. They produce a substance that prevents molting. When they stop secreting, the crab molts. Cutting off the eyestalks will cause the crab to molt continuously.

Some of Sally's relatives get really large. The Japanese crab may grow to twelve feet across. The Atlantic lobster reaches two feet long and weighs thirty-four pounds. Sally, though, is only about four inches from front to back and eight inches from side to side.

Here in the islands she and her crab relatives are important tidal-zone scavengers. Sally will eat almost anything animal or vegetable, dead or alive. About a hundred feet from where I'm sitting watching Sally, I found a complete skeleton of a marine iguana, every bone in place and attached to a neighboring one by cartilage. Sally and her kin had picked every shred of flesh from the dead animal. The skeleton was so nicely crab-cleaned, sun-bleached, and whitened, that I saved it for later mounting and study.

Looking closely at Sally I see a pair of fanlike structures just beneath the base of her eyestalks that are beating so fast they're just a blur of motion. They are her gill bailers. Underwater her eight pairs of gills extract oxygen directly from the water. Water enters through two cross slits on the front of her abdomen, flows over the gills, and leaves by two openings just beneath her mouth. The gill bailers literally pull the water through the openings and swish it out in a steady forward stream. When Sally comes out of the water onto the rocks, she must breathe air. Now her gill bailers reverse direction and pull air into the two gill chambers where the ever-moist gills extract the oxygen. The crab is equally at home in the sea or on land.

I stand up. Instantly Sally darts sideways over

the edge of the rock toward the water. When I walk toward her, she jumps into the sea. Through the crystal clear water I watch her scuttle to the bottom. Her rear pair of legs, flattened like paddles, flick in and out. After she disappears under a boulder, I sigh with pleasure and turn away. You and I have had another short glimpse of the life and ways of one of God's creatures here in the Galápagos Islands. We, like Darwin, marvel at nature's various ways. Unlike Darwin, though, we praise God for His ingenious creative power in giving us the Sally Lightfoot crabs.

Darwin's Finches

"I think it's a large ground finch."

"No, it's a cactus ground finch."

Neither of us was really sure which species of Darwin's famous finches we looked at. At least five different species of finches ate the rice Dr. Ernest Booth and I threw down at our feet.

We stood just outside our kitchen door, busily picking out seeds, stones, beetles, and rat manure so we could cook the rice for breakfast. Although it was our daily morning chore, it wasn't a boring job, because we could purposely spill some rice on the ground for the birds.

Fifty or sixty birds had discovered how to get a

free meal by showing up at our house on Santa Cruz Island every morning. We enjoyed trying to figure out which species was which among the milling black-and-mottled-brown birds.

Just to look at Darwin's finches you wouldn't be impressed with them. They're not particularly attractive. But without a doubt they're the most famous group of birds in the whole history of biology. Some species are black all over, and the rest look like any female house sparrow to the unaware observer. In fact, all thirteen species resemble and act more like house sparrows than anything else. Some are slightly bigger than others, some have larger, heavier finch-type beaks, and others have pointed, slender beaks.

An author considers no book on evolution complete today unless it devotes several pages to the Darwin finches with illustrations to show all the variations from species to species. Large numbers of the birds occur on all of the larger islands in the Galápagos Archipelago.

It was only after returning to England following his famous round-the-world voyage on the H.M.S. *Beagle* that Darwin had time to analyze his collection of the birds that now bear his name. They seemed to him to offer evidence that disproved the separate creation of animal species. He reasoned that if the special-creation theory is true, then it was a strange coincidence of creation to find thirteen similar species of finches existing only in the Galápagos Islands.

He was right. At that time many people believed that God had created each new species right where man found it. Darwin couldn't accept that idea. From his study of the finches, giant tortoises, and other animals in the Galápagos Islands, he developed the idea that each new species found only there had developed from some ancestor that came out from the mainland soon after the formation of the island.

Darwin reasoned that newly arrived finches would be able to change to fit the particular circumstances of each island. Later the new species would spread to the nearest neighbor islands, and then several species would be able to live in harmony since they had developed different-type beaks to fit their various feeding habits.

Today we accept Darwin's conclusion about the finches' immediate origin, but we can't agree with Darwin when he proposes that both finches and marine iguanas had the same ancestor at some time in the distant past. Each originated from its own creature type. The evidence of change in both is real, but the degree of change is a theoretical point of argument.

How have the finches changed? One group, the ground finches, have large, heavy, curved beaks like the American cardinal and grosbeak. They feed mainly on seeds and sometimes insects. Another group, the cactus finches, have sharper, more pointed beaks, and they eat the tiny developing seed tissues of the cactus flowers. A third group, the tree finches, consume insects dug out of woody tissues of trees with their curved and somewhat slender beaks.

The woodpecker and mangrove finches have

heavy, straight beaks for probing and chiseling their way into woody places where insects conceal themselves. The two finches are famous for using long cactus spines to probe and dig insect larvae out of deep holes in the trees—one of those rare cases where an animal makes and uses a tool. Furthermore, if the tool is a good one, the bird saves it to employ again and again. A pair of woodpecker finches in captivity feeding on mealworms (a kind of beetle larva) would deliberately hide the worms and then dig them out with their spiny tools, not just once but several times as though practicing.

The vegetarian finch has a short, straight, heavy bill that fits a variety of foods. It eats buds, leaves, flowers, fruits, and seeds. The warbler finch has a delicate bill similar to our insect-eating warblers in America. Small insects are its primary food.

Although each species of Darwin finch has its own special type of beak that fits it for its own special food, they share a lot of the same kind of diet. Since food is abundant, they don't seem to have to compete for it.

The Darwin finches have no regular enemies except for house cats introduced into the islands. The birds are so tame that cats easily catch them.

Some finches have strange habits indeed. The sharp-beaked ground finch on Wenman Island will hop onto a masked booby's back and peck at the soft skin at the base of the bird's wing feathers until they bleed. Then the finch feeds on the oozing blood. Strangely, the booby doesn't seem to mind. Sometimes it will swing its beak around at the finch as if shooing a fly, but the finch just keeps on.

Some Darwin finches will flock around a booby nest where a chick loudly begs food from its parents. When the parent regurgitates the food, the finches eat it before the young booby. Other finches will pick parasitic insects off the boobies.

A few will eat Sally Lightfoot crabs in the soft-shell stage after molting. Some feed on the carcasses of dead sea lions. Others will surround a swallow-tailed gull egg and take turns hammering it with their beaks until the egg breaks. Then all drink the contents. Still others will lever a man-o'-war bird's egg off the side of its nest so it will fall to the ground below and break. The Darwin finches will pretty much eat any food available besides that for which they are apparently specialized to eat.

Male finches of most species will build two or three nests, then hang around each nest twittering and twitching in a courtship display to attract a female. Once pairing takes place, the female picks out one of the domed nests and lays her eggs. The dome over the nest shades the eggs from the tropical sun when both of the birds are away feeding.

The Darwin finches chatter noisily wherever they congregate, totally unconcerned about anything going on about them. Their appearance and habits helped inspire Charles Darwin's theory of evolution. What a pity that Darwin jumped to far bigger conclusions than he should have.

Patient, careful study of nature will lead the student to God rather than away from Him. Nature is really a revelation of God's order and creative intelligence. May His glory be magnified through an understanding of His creatures.

The Galápagos Swallow-tailed Gull

The deep blue waters of the Pacific break with a never-ending crash on the volcanic rocks far below where I'm sitting. Within a pebble's toss is a family of masked boobies around their nest, a pair of marine iguanas basking on a rock, a female lava lizard with her pink throat flashing in the sunlight, and a pair of swallow-tailed gulls worrying over a single bluish-white, brown-speckled egg in a nest of small pebbles. Each of the widely different Galápagos animals exists in the presence of the others in perfect harmony. None fear me.

The boobies take turns feeding their big nestling. The marine iguanas sleep on. The lava lizard darts up on the toe of my shoe and snaps a fly off my ankle. The two swallow-tailed gulls chatter to each other as though trying to decide whose turn it is to go eat and whose turn to watch over the single camouflaged egg. The only thing different from yesterday, last week, last year, last decade, last century—indeed, the last thousand years—is I'm here too. The timeless quality of the Galápagos Islands and all of their special plants and animals is their most-loved characteristic. The illusion is almost perfect that nothing grows old. Only the mummified body of a pelican or the gray bleached shell of a giant tortoise remind us that death respects neither animal nor man. Isaiah's picture of a land where the lamb and lion lie down together is yet to come. But the little sample of peace and harmony surrounding my feet whets my appetite for a world made new. I anxiously wait to explore that world too.

Easily the most handsome bird in the Galápagos Islands, the swallow-tailed gull is also the most attractive gull in the world. Scattered all through the islands, the beautiful bird lives in colonies with the boobies in the high cliffs along the shorelines. One can recognize the swallow-tail in flight by the large triangular white patch on its long wings. It is the only sea gull with a definite forked tail. A dark gray hood covers its head and neck. Most of the body is a soft neutral gray. Its throat and breast have a rosy tinge. The main wing feathers are black, and the tail is white. A showy crimson eyelid rings the large brown eye. The webbed feet are a dusky pink. The swallow-tail always looks neat and trim, more like a tern than a gull. Sea gulls are to the seas what the vultures are to the land—scavengers on dead animals and scraps left over from the feeding of other creatures.

The larger, more abundant species of gulls are the most vulturelike in keeping the seas cleaned of dead animal matter. The Galápagos swallow-tail, however, feeds mostly on small fish scooped off the sea surface at night. They also consume surface-swimming squid. Like most night creatures, the gull's eyes shine in the dark from reflected light.

All gulls wander far and wide in solitary migration flights that occur at any time of the year. The swallow-tail often shows up six hundred to a thousand miles away from the Galápagos, along the coasts of Ecuador and Chile. The most famous gull migration was the historical arrival of thousands of them in the Salt Lake City area—far from the sea—just as a plague of locusts, now called the Mormon crickets, threatened to wipe out the Mormons' crops. In gratitude to the bird, the Mormons erected a monument in Salt Lake City to the sea gull. It since has become the state bird of Utah.

During the daytime a pair of swallow-tails will hang around the nest to protect the single egg from the swooping raids of the man-o'-war birds. Each shares in incubating the egg. At night, if both birds fly off to feed together, the egg may disappear down the gullet of the short-eared owl. Dark down covers the newly hatched chick except for a white head which shows up at night like a beacon to guide the parents returning to the nest from their feeding expedition. Other gull chicks are usually a uniform brown. The parent birds each have a grayish-white mark at the tip of their bills which the young birds can see at night and continually peck at. The pecking stimulates the parent bird to give up food to the chick.

The lava cliffs of the swallow-tail's nesting site have lots of rocks and crevices into which the young gull can hide to escape a raiding man-o'-war bird.

Adult swallow-tailed gulls make loud clicking sounds in addition to their high-pitched piercing cries. The clicks may be a way of "echolocating" their nests at night, working something like the bats' radar.

Male swallow-tails have no loud raucous call to advertise their presence to a mate. Instead, the male quietly picks out a nest site, gathers small stone fragments to make a little ring on the ground, then waits for a female to alight nearby and accept his offer.

In the air, the swallow-tail's body pulses up and down with each beat of the strong wings. The smooth, unruffled, streamlined body reminds us of a jet piercing the sky with great power and beauty as it passes by.

With the beautiful swallow-tailed gull we bring our book to a close. Darwin's islands—so important to the evolutionary theory—have in reality inspired us with nature's marvels of adaptation. Each animal and each plant specialized in its own manner to survive in this bleak, dry, hostile environment. God in His all-wise way put in each form of life the ability to adjust to circumstances almost too rugged for life. But we have also seen that no animal changes into anything other than a special form of that same animal.

We, too, have our adaptations for survival in a hostile, sin-damaged world. Every time Satan's ingenuity produces a new disease-causing organism, God leads man to discover an antibiotic or some other means of keeping us alive just a little longer. God is anticipating that we will come to our senses, recognize the conflict between good and evil both in nature and in the lives of man, and thus realize that our hope for the future is only in him. Then we can look forward to an entire world made into a Galápagos Eden without the hardships. "All nature in its surpassing loveliness will offer to God a constant tribute of praise and adoration. The world will be bathed in the light of heaven" (*Ministry of Healing*, p. 506).